Chris
with best wishes
&

NOD WHISPERS

keep

Peter

by

PETER NEILSON

GW00722402

Since the massive interest caused by the novel and film called "The Horse Whisperer" and subsequent publicised work by the likes of Monty Roberts and Linda Tellington-Jones there is great interest by the horse world universally and the general public in communicating with and healing animals. This is a true "Black Beauty" story and tells the story of Nod, a mentally traumatised horse, unable to behave normally and his life and times. The other essential character in this dramatic story is Peter Neilson, a Scotsman, a trained engineer and former farmer, whose conventional life from a farming background always included horses and dogs. A professional horseman and retired Joint Master of the Duke of Buccleuch's Hunt in the beautiful Scottish Borders. Trainer and Healer of Horses.

Join Peter and Nod on a journey of discovery, healing and spectacular transformation. Peter's work has been the subject of much Media interest across the United Kingdom and beyond and has featured on BBC, Channel 4, Border TV and the printed media.

The Horses' Prayer

From Richard Wilson, Ontario.

To Thee, my Master, I offer my prayer. Feed me, water and care for me and when the days work is done, provide me with shelter, a clean dry bed and a stall wide enough for me to lie down in comfort.

Always be kind to me. Talk to me. Your voice often means as much to me as the reins. Pet me sometimes, so that I may serve you more gladly and learn to love you. Do not jerk the reins and do not whip me going uphill. Never strike, beat or kick me when I do not understand what you want, but give me a chance to understand you. Watch me, and if I fail to do your bidding, see if something is wrong with my tack or feet.

Do not check me so that I cannot have the free use of my head. If you insist that I wear blinkers, so that I cannot see behind me as it was intended I should. I pray you be careful that the blinkers stand well out from my eyes.

Do not overload me, or hitch me where water will drip on me. Keep me well shod. Examine my teeth when I do not eat. I may have an ulcerated tooth and that, you know, is very painful. Do not tie, or fix my head in an unnatural position.

I cannot tell you when I am thirsty, so give me clean, cool water often. I cannot tell you in words when I am sick, so watch me, that by signs you may know my condition. Give me all possible shelter from the hot sun and put a blanket on me, not when I am working, but when I am standing in the cold. Never put a frosty bit in my mouth, first warm it by holding it a moment in your hands.

I try to carry you and your burdens without a murmur and wait patiently for you long hours of the day and night. Without the power to choose my shoes or patch, my feet sometimes fall on difficult places which I often pray may give a safe and sure footing Remember that I must be ready at any moment to lose my life in your service.

And finally, O my Master, when my useful strength has gone, do not turn me out graze, or sell me to some cruel owner, to be slowly tortured and starved to death; but thou, my Master, take my life in the kindest way and your God will reward you here and hereafter. You will not consider me irrelevant if I ask this in the name of him who was born in a stable.

Foreword

You are about to embark on a wondrous journey. Nod's story is a remarkable one, a pilgrimage to a sacred place - that of wholeness. As you read this, you will learn of Nod's lifetimes filled with hardship, pain, suffering and trauma. You will read how Peter became aware of other horses' traumas as Nod's story unfolded. However, this book isn't about pain and suffering. It is about how lifetimes of pain can be transmuted and healed when humans and horses come together to heal.

Peter Neilson's perseverance and commitment to this beautiful horse is an inspiration. What began as a simple question of solving a horse's "behavior problem," evolved into the incredible journey into wholeness for both the man and the horse. The path was fraught with strange and unusual twists and turns. Peter, a practical, no nonsense, down-to-earth fellow was drawn into experiencing non-physical realities and past life experiences perhaps never dreamed of. Still, he persevered, never giving up on finding a way to help Nod, no matter how weird or "way out" the option appeared to be! If something or anything gave another clue into Nod's problem, Peter enthusiastically followed the lead until it ran out or led to another clue. The man and the horse had much in common!

I had the honor of being Nod's voice on occasions so that Peter could hear Nod's thoughts and feelings. I was struck by this great horse's great heart, by his deep desire to find a way out of his predicaments, for his huge ability to trust, to keep trying, to go on and on, no matter how challenging the course or invisible the path. In my years working with horses I've learned that they carry the quality of idealism, which is defined as "persistent hopefulness." Nod's idealism and Peter's determination to find the answers allowed them both to experience partnership and trust that was much greater than man and horse. It was the partnership between two old souls, souls who had been friends and partners before, but who needed each other in a new way this time around. At the bottom of it all was a great love between these two beings. This love allowed them both to transcend pain and lifetimes to discover something very beautiful.

I invite you to experience this incredible journey and to ask yourself how Nod and Peter's "ride" can inspire you in your own life - with humans and with animals. If you're lucky enough to have a horse in your life, think hard about how and why you came together. Perhaps Nod's story will inspire you to embark on your own healing journey - together. With love all things are possible.

Kate Solisti-Mattelon
Boulder, Colorado
February 2004

Introduction

NOD

Nod arrived at the farm near Kelso where I live, in the summer of 1993, it did not take long to find out that he suffered from extremely complex and difficult to diagnose physical and mental problems.

Nod and I say thank you to Lavender Dower, Morag MacDonald-Worsley and Kate Solisti-Mattelon, a very, very big thank you. I also thank Alistair Murdoch, Judith Hampson, Doug Watts of Jacqui Bennett Writers Bureau and Margaret Hay, who had to put up with a dyslectic, computer-ignorant horseman.

Horses are my life. From an early age, I realised I had greater empathy with and love of animals than other children and this carried into adulthood. But Nod was to send me on a journey.

The first half of my childhood was at Chapleton in Ayrshire, where my parents soon learnt to give up worrying when I was missing from the house, even though it was easy for a child to get lost in the surrounding woods. I would have as companions the housedogs, in particular the black Labrador Cuckie, who was my shadow. I would be either with the ponies, the Hunters or the big gentle giants, the Clydesdales. Then there were the coal pit ponies, who on their one annual holiday came up from the deep dark pits to see daylight, smell clean air, feel the wind and the rain, roll, stretch, yawn, scratch, drink from the burn, eat grass and have some sun on their backs. I was warned not to go near the people from the coal pits, because they didn't like children and they had a tendency to kick and bite at opposite ends, but I paid no heed and was always off to see and talk to these new friends.

The second half of my childhood was at Monksford in Roxburghshire, between the Eildon hills and the river Tweed. Here a large part of my time was spent on the backs of ponies, often bareback and occasionally without a bridle, sticking my fingers into the side of their mouths to steer them. I rode the Eildon Hills and the riverbanks day in day out - this was cowboys and Indians for real.

With the help of a Labrador, a toy poodle and a miniature dachshund, I used to hunt the foxes along the riverbanks. The foxes were very helpful when they got too far ahead of me, they would sit down waiting until I caught up, before moving on. That boy was close enough, they would say. I was fascinated by nature, by the animal kingdom, by the birds of prey, the little kestrel quivering on high, the barn owl silently gliding by, the foxes and the dogs hunting. I hunt with both weapons and in partnership with animals.

I had twenty unsuccessful years working in engineering, a career I was forced into, followed by eight enjoyable years farming before the weather bust me. Now, having reached the age when I qualify for cheap travel, though there are no trains in this lovely part of southeast Scotland, I have two jobs, one as part of the management team running the local hunt, the other as a horse whisperer. Both have developed from my affinity with nature and allow me to communicate with and heal animals, principally the horse.

Table of Contents

The Horses' Prayer v

Foreword vii

Introduction ix

Chapter 1
Ebony moves on, purchase of Nod 1

Chapter 2
*Nod meets the other horses, introduction of
Lavender Dower* 7

Chapter 3
Introduction of Kate Solisti 20

Chapter 4
Introduction of TTEAM 25

Chapter 5
Introduction of Morag MacDonald-Worsley ... 33

Chapter 6
Other complimentary therapies 39

Chapter 7
Milly arrives 48

Chapter 8

Morris arrives 55

Chapter 9

Nod visits TTEAM farm and the seaside 69

Chapter 10

Milly's problems 78

Chapter 11

Nod release from his trauma 83

Chapter 12

Cats and Quizzy arrive 90

Chapter 13

Nod and I are a centaur 105

Chapter 14

The spirit World's celebration to honour Nod ... 108

Glossary 112

Maps 117

Ebony stepping over a 3 feet square box fence

Chapter 1

Ebony moves on, purchase of Nod

It is often said that you have only one 'special' horse in your lifetime. I have been honoured to have several, Ebony was one of them. Before he joined my team of horses, his previous owners had tried to make a living out of him as a showjumper, completely destroying his confidence in the process. The dealer's daughter from whom I bought him had very quietly worked with him for a year, slowly allowing him to recover. Ebony was a lovely, gentle giant of a horse, black with white points. Until then my horses had been no bigger than 16.2/16.3 hands. Here was this fellow, fully 17.3. I had no saddle, girth, rugs or bridle big enough for him. His neck seemed to go on forever and my reins were all a mile too short.

We had such fun together out hunting. Cruising slowly across country, other horses were galloping hard to keep up. He seemed to step over five bar gates with ease and we often jumped some very big obstacles. Sadly, though an infection in the marrow had split a bone and he had to be put down in the spring of 1993. And I can't help it - no matter how often something like this happens, no matter how many dogs and horses I've seen undergo a similar fate I am in floods of tears every time.

All the same, I was short of a horse to make up the team required for my job as a field master and as usual, I knew that this would probably require me having to drive long distances to inspect any new horse that might meet my specifications. I decided to organise a trip to examine several at one go.

Although horses are herd animals, I am always looking for the herd leaders, horses who have fire in their bellies, the natural front runners, who will want to take charge, be bold and fast. They also have to be physically well built, strong with good bone. Rarely do thoroughbred horses match up to this, as they are unable to withstand the workload.

So, I set about organising a trip of several hundred miles to inspect a number of horses. Ten days later I left home near Kelso, my dogs accompanying me. Sometimes the motor seemed no more than a mobile kennel. . .

I went to Northumberland and looked at two horses in that county, but neither fitted the bill. So I carried on down the A1 to my next stop, in Yorkshire. When I turned off the main road and arrived at the dealer's yard, I was greeted by the sight of a lovely old stone farmhouse, with behind it a stone steading converted into stables and two grass paddocks. The dealer welcomed me into the house, where I relaxed for a while, chatting and eating a large piece of sponge cake with a nice cup of tea. Suitably refreshed, we went to the stables via the tack room, where everything was immaculate, all the buttons and buckles polished and twinkling, all the leather waxed and shining, with that lovely aroma of saddle soap. As I walked down the swept passage between the boxes, I glanced at the horses on either side. The dealer stopped at the end right-hand box and pointed in.

"This one's called 'Nod'," he said.

I looked into the box. A bright bay quality gelding stood there, about 16.2 hands with a shiny coat and a big white blaze down the front of his face. His clear eyes studied me placidly.

"How old?" I asked the dealer. An eight-year-old, I was told.

I opened the door and walked into his box, which was filled with a thick covering of clean wheat straw. I examined the horse thoroughly, to absorb as much detail as possible - his size, conformation, bone, shortness of back, strength, aura -the package. That completed, I moved to him and ran my hands over his body feeling for bumps and knocks - any signs of old injuries. He had a good frame, bone, shaped hooves, clean limbs, one with a little scar and a kind, clear, bright eye. This could be just the horse I was looking for. A quality hunter with a dash of Clydesdale in his ancestry. So I asked the dealer if he could be tacked up for me.

Whilst his daughter was doing this, the dealer and I walked out to the larger of the two paddocks, about ten acres in size, with some old hunter-trial type fences in it. We talked about cabbages and kings, waiting for Nod. When he arrived, Nod was in high fettle, blowing in his nostrils, prancing, foaming slightly at his mouth, definitely a mettlesome horse. This was quite some horse. The aura he threw was terrific. He was definitely his own person. I know all horses have different characters, as do all humans, but his presence announced, "I am that I am." It was simply the way he stood, the way he looked and the way he held himself, inspecting the world.

The daughter tried to ride him around quietly, but it was obvious that she was apprehensive so I decided to ride Nod. Before I mounted up I asked about the extraordinary wooden bit in his mouth, the likes of which I had never seen. I got a mumbled, bland answer, which explained nothing. I got on Nod for the first time and just walked around, feeling all the messages coming from him. What a horse! He exuded power. As he had a very fast walk, he would have a similar very fast gallop. He had some fire in his belly. His extended trot was amazing - with his front legs stretched out, nearly horizontal - he covered the ground fast. With excitement and a twinge of nervousness I popped him over some fences. *Jiminy crickets! Could this fellow jump!* Boldness, power... phenomenal.

Eventually I got off and handed Nod back to the daughter to return him to the stables. If you walk into a garage and say I want to drive that Ferrari, take it out onto a track, open the car up - power, smouldering exhilarating power - that was Nod. He was going to be no armchair ride.

I turned to the dealer and asked how much he wanted? The price was expensive, but not too high for a horse required to control a big galloping 'field' the collective name for a crowd of horses out hunting.

"OK," I said, "I'll let you know."

I got into the car and set off. Out of sight of the dealer's yard, I stopped so that the dogs and I could spend a penny, then motored on to stay with friends that night in Lincolnshire.

I looked at more horses as I travelled south, then I cut through the Midlands so that I could travel north on the west side of the UK, visiting other establishments. I had inspected and ridden a horse in a yard in Cheshire, from where I had previously obtained a successful horse. This one was of a similar stamp and age to Nod, very comfortable to ride and workmanlike, but just a shade inferior in all attributes and cheaper. I was about to shake hands to complete the deal, when Nod sprang into my mind - A flash of instinct? A nudge from a guardian angel? Divine intervention? Whatever it was at that moment I knew that Nod was destined to be my horse.

I returned to the car and started for home. I stopped on the M6, rang and cancelled the last appointment and had some supper. With a sigh of relief I told the dogs that we were heading home and that everyone could sleep in their own beds tonight, which for them, meant armchairs.

The next day I rang the dealer in Yorkshire. "I'll take Nod," I told him "I'll arrange for the local horse transporting firm to uplift him." He asked when the vet would come to inspect him, but I replied, that wouldn't be necessary. Over the years I have inspected horses in different yards, and know instinctively whether I liked them or not. The problem is, that I can't always read what is inside the horse. But Nod physically satisfied my specification, so I forwarded the correct money and Nod was collected the next week.

Nod

Lucy

Chapter 2

Nod meets the other horses, introduction of Lavender Dower

Nod went out into the field with my other horses - Ben, JoJo, and Lucy Glitters - for three weeks, during which time he put on some condition, making me wonder if the grass was better here than in Yorkshire. The hillside field where they spend their summer holidays gave them about seven acres of grazing, but it was relatively steep - as much as one-in-one in places - with the water trough at the bottom. A large tree gave plenty of shade at the top, where the breeze kept the flies at bay. All in all, this environment was exactly right for keeping their muscles hard and they are able to put on condition, their fat been converted into additional brawn. When their holidays were over they would start the process of getting fit with slow roadwork to harden their legs.

They came in on the first day of July to prepare for hunting. The farrier, Dave, came over from St. Boswells, and Alec the dentist paid a visit from Edinburgh, each of them doing their stuff. The horses also commenced homeopathic preventative treatment for flu, tetanus and worms.

Timing was everything during this period - the horses were getting a little bored lounging around in the field with nothing to do, so preparing them for hunting offered them welcome new challenges. But as the horses' holiday came to an end, the local schoolchildren are delighted to begin theirs - plenty of help to be had there, if necessary.

Initial training consisted of walking the roads for ten days - about an hour each day. This would be increased to an hour and a half of walking and trotting, bumped up to two hours by the fourth week, with a lot of slow trotting uphill, all on roads. Luckily, here in the Tweed valley, a beautiful part of southeast Scotland, the single width public roads carry very little traffic.

The procession sets out every morning from the stables: four horses, four dogs, with the number of horses actually ridden depending on how many jockeys turned up. And so we travelled the country lanes - Fern, an elderly black Labrador, and Rambo, a little old brown lurcher, usually mooching about close by, inspecting all the new overnight smells, while Fern's daughter Jay was striding out briskly, and Bizzy, another lurcher with a ruff on his neck, travelling parallel to us, several hundred yards to one side. The gently rolling landscape provided the perfect setting, rich woodland interspersed with an abundance of mature trees, situated amidst hills and a variety of prominent landmarks, many of historic significance with the Cheviot Hills themselves completing the backdrop.

And - dear Lord - the wondrous diversity of Nature! Wild flowers, delicate whispy grasses, wild strawberries (their flavour out of this world!), wild raspberries and gooseberries coming on, brambles, delicious wild cherries that can be picked from horseback - a veritable feast. The skylarks trilling above, whaups (curlews to you non-Scots), oystercatchers, peesies (peewits) - the adults and young of so many species were there to see, all going about their business, unconcerned by our passage.

Heaven? Well, yes, up to a point. But once I started to work with Nod, I soon found a few cracks in this celestial perfection. For a start, he was not the easiest of horses to exercise.

Nod expected to move fast, irrespective of whether I was riding him or leading him and as for a child or someone inexperienced riding him - no way. The moment I was in the saddle, he was permanently pulling to go faster, froth and foam spewing from his mouth, often with his tongue sticking out to the right by ten inches.

Even when he was being led, he'd yank hard on the rope, trying to go flat out regardless of the other horses. In effect, he was continually attempting to bolt. Part of the problem, I knew, was what the dentist had found. Nod's teeth had been sorted, but his mouth was a mass of scars, scar tissue and ulcers. This was going to take some time to heal and it no doubt partly explained why the dealer had been using a wooden bit. But the biggest problem by far was mental. Nod had no self-control - he simply wanted to bolt.

I had for many years worked with Lavender Dower, who had practised Radionics for the past fifty years and started 'The Institute of Complimentary Medicines'. Radionics is a remarkable holistic therapy, which works to stimulate the body's natural self-healing powers. One of the key beliefs upon which Radionics is founded is that every individual has a unique energy pattern, as characteristic as a thumbprint. These patterns can be distorted and thrown into disharmony by psychological states, viruses, bacterial influences and injuries. The aim of radionic therapy is to detect and analyse these patterns, to remove or reverse the original causes of the patient's illness, and to open up the channels for the life force to flow freely - a form of medical dowsing.

Lavender had a very successful practice, specialising in the treatment of horses, and was able to care for up to a thousand equine patients at any one time. Her success rate was as high as eighty per cent, even though vets had often advised that many of the horses referred to her had no option other than to be put down.

Years ago, I suffered a nasty infection after being hospitalised for an operation. The infection had seen off all antibiotics, so I decided to try homeopathic and herbal medicines. So successful were these that I was an immediate convert, and I'd since ensured that the vet I used was trained in both complimentary and conventional medicine, with the proviso to use the techniques of the former wherever possible.

When a new horse arrives, I take a small piece of its mane and post it off to Lavender, along with a list of all the horse's known quirks and a straightforward description of its appearance. This had been done for Nod. From now onwards I would ring Lavender at least twice a week while Nod was in work. This was one patient that was going to need a lot of discussion, it seemed.

As it turned out, he was going to test us to our limits, and if it had not been for Lavender's support, patience and comfort, I doubt that I could have coped and seen it through. Nod was to be my supreme challenge.

In August we had three mornings cub hunting up on the heather-clad hills to the west of Hawick and Selkirk. Late summer is a glorious time to be there. The tranquillity of the surroundings is marvellous, giving one the impression that the whole world is at peace. The views across miles of rolling hills, constantly folding into one another to form hidden valleys, are spoilt only by the knowledge that many of these hills are now covered in uniform monotonous blanket forestry, the same process that has devastated wildlife, both on land and in the watercourses. On the remaining hills the heather is in full bloom at this time of year, its pollen filling the air with perfume. And every time we all ride up this way, somewhere in these many square miles of heather I will find a clump of white heather. Dismounting, I make sure to pick a sprig for each person with me, certain in the knowledge that there is still plenty left for the spirits of the land.

But in that August, it became instantly apparent during these morning expeditions that Nod, although obviously exceptionally powerful, bold and fast, had no self-control. Arriving at the meeting point, I would find the floor of the trailer was covered in spew and foam from Nod's mouth. When he was at the walk, all was well: he was observing and behaving like any normal horse, albeit an exceptionally keen one. But ask him to trot, canter or gallop, and he would try to bolt, going faster and faster, usually in an unwaveringly straight line, with no regard for the terrain he was crossing - it was as if his brain ceased to function and he became a run away train. He had no self-preservation, this made him almost impossible to ride, of course; he was a real danger, both to himself and to me. I normally ride horses in a snaffle, but no matter what bit I tried him in; the result was the same - no joy. On top of this, because his mouth was in such a mess, the old injuries bled and often his tongue stuck out of his mouth nine to ten inches to the right. He appeared incapable of listening, of considering what he was doing, and he paid no attention to any communication from my hands, legs, voice or thought.

Under normal circumstances I would have got rid of Nod. He was completely unsuitable for this job, or any other. He was a disaster and dangerous. But the horse had some mysterious hold over me, something I cannot explain to this day, and which first became apparent on the day when Nod sprang into my mind, as I was about to buy the horse in Cheshire instead of him. I knew now that not merely was I going to keep him, but I was duty bound to do everything possible to help this wonderful horse overcome his mental trauma.

I will never forget Sunday 29th August 1993. It had been a lovely sunny day, I went to fetch the horses in that evening, and I found Nod in dire trouble. He was in so much pain he could barely move. Leaving all the field gates open, hoping he would follow I brought the other horses into the stables and then went back for Nod. He had moved desperately slowly but eventually we made it to the stables.

I rang for the duty vet and luckily one of my own vets, Tim, was on call that weekend. He arrived as fast as he could. Nod had the most violent crippling stomach pains and moved in a way that suggested he was suffering from cramp. The examination included the drawing-off of fluid by a needle and syringe from his intestines, and phone calls to the 'Dick Vet' the Royal (Dick) School of Veterinary Studies at the Bush near Edinburgh. This well-known veterinary establishment was run under the auspices of Edinburgh University and used by local vets as the referral centre for serious cases.

As always, a SOS phone call went to Lavender Dower. I briefly explained the situation and told her that Tim couldn't find the cause, but a problem had shown up in the fluid drawn off from his stomach; it is all wrong. I let her know that Tim was at the moment talking again to the Dick Vet, requesting that he be booked in at once. Lavender said she would dash upstairs to her treatment room and consult her instruments immediately. She rang back a little later to say that, so far, her analysis showed Nod was suffering from a massive infection of the stomach. She had begun treatment straightaway, she told me.

Nod was given a gigantic dose of painkiller injected into a vein so that he would be able to withstand the pain caused by movement in transit. He was loaded into the trailer, and then transported to the Dick Vet, where two vets rushed him into the operating theatre. I sat outside, a very worried man. Eventually, a surgeon appeared and gave me the diagnosis - Nod was suffering from peritonitis. This had been caused by an enormous infestation of worms, which had perforated his gut in several places. He stayed there for five days whilst they treated him and then I fetched him home for further treatment. After four long and anxious weeks, Nod at last recovered and was back out hunting.

By then another trait had become apparent, Nod's consumption of food was astronomical. In the stall next door to him was Ben, a similar sized, mousy coloured, dark bay Irish gelding, with no white markings, a solid framed horse with good bone, strong and very workmanlike. He had once been a registered show jumper going by the name of Seren, but lacked in thoroughbred blood compared to Nod. Nevertheless, he quickly became Nod's best pal, a shoulder to cry on, as it were and main support, seemingly sharing in Nod's trials and tribulations. Ben was a very laid back fellow. To him, life was about eating, sleeping, resting and hunting. He was, however not keen on the fitness routine. In his eyes, ten days of boring roadwork was an ample suffficiency - you could see that all he wanted to do was to get on with the proper business and stop wasting his time and effort. Out hunting he woke up.

Ben earned himself a nickname - 'The Irish Oaf' - because he adored watching hounds and was always so enthralled by them hunting, speaking and casting that he never, ever, looked where he was putting his feet. On the hills we have small open surface drains, approximately nine inches wide by nine inches deep and spaced about eighteen feet apart. Most horses learn to adjust their stride when galloping over them, but not Ben. It was bad enough on white hills ie grass covered where they were visible, but on heather hills - oh dear! On more than one occasion, we both found out what a good landing pad deep heather is. But Ben was first-class to field master on; there was no way that he would tolerate any horse in front of him. He was a natural herd leader, with a good turn of speed and the ability, boldness and desire to jump anything. He loved everything to do with hunting, and was so undemanding in the stables that he was a pleasure to look after and work with, a thoroughly straightforward, unsophisticated, kind character.

Nod's appetite was quite extraordinary - he ate twice as much hay as Ben. As a result he drank vast quantities of water and was forever staleing (passing urine), which was not good for his kidneys. It had also become apparent that his hooves didn't grow, which was to cause considerable problems over the winter when being shod. For all his vast consumption of hay, he was not absorbing protein properly and so it was evident that his body was very badly run down. The road to recovery was going to be painfully slow. Worrying, too, were the indications that Nod never lay down to sleep, neither in the stables nor in the field. There was never any sign of compressed straw where a body had flattened it, and although the other horses were seen lying down in the field, never Nod. All horse have a locking mechanism in their joints so they can sleep standing up, thus ready for instant flight, but never to lie down at all to take the weight off their feet and legs is very exceptional and unnatural. Why was Nod unable to lie down?

As this winter progressed, another problem reared its head. Nod was not responding to any medicines, be they conventional, herbal or homeopathic. This was not a total surprise, as he wasn't benefiting from the astronomical quantities of food he was consuming.

It was now obvious that his body thermostat was not functioning correctly - Nod was ultra-sensitive to wet or cold. When you put your hands on a horse's ears, you can gauge the temperature of its whole body. If the ears are cold and you massage them until they become warm, then you know that their whole body is warm.

Gee whiz, this lad's body was one big wreck. Never mind his mental state.

When riding Nod, either at home or out hunting, he reacted as if he had been overraced. It was a bit like driving a car when the accelerator becomes stuck - the engine overrevs, and you're unable to slow. The only way the car will stop is to switch off the engine. Nod was reacting in a similar style, his brain appeared to be programmed only to go flat out. This can happen when the horse is being raced and becomes so exhausted that its brain is unable to recover and stays in a locked condition. With Nod being so fast and bold, had someone early in his life tried to take advantage of this by team chasing him? I couldn't help thinking of those tales of heroic horses that had run beyond the point of exhaustion so that a messenger could deliver some dire warning. Nod did not respond to any remedial therapy.

Obviously previous riders must have experienced these problems with Nod, evidenced by the injuries to his mouth, which were clearly a result of their effort to control him. His mouth bled under the slightest pressure of the bit, so I switched to riding him in a hackamore, a bitless bridle. This works by exerting pressure on the bridge of the nose. Unfortunately I found that he did not respond to that either. His nostrils could be flattened and still he paid no attention. The first hackamore broke while out hunting, and I was left with a horse galloping flat out and only a neck strap to hang on to! With the next hackamore, I tried using running reins as well; these afforded me considerably increased leverage while reducing the number of times I would have to apply pressure to Nod's nose. Regrettably, not only did this not help, but it also flattened his nostrils further, so perhaps insuffficient air was getting to his brain, compounding the problem. There again, it seemed as though Nod's brain didn't function in the first place.

After much trial and error, I eventually found a bit that seemed to suit Nod, one designed by the well-known American horsewoman and trainer, Linda Tellington Jones. Though it looked severe, if not fearsome, with an excessive bar length to take the double reins, the cross bar had an acorn in its port and had been cranked at an angle, so this bit's action was gentle.

I had a choice when out hunting on Nod: we could either meander about or charge full steam ahead in a flat-out gallop. There was no happy medium of gently trotting or cantering. In charge mode his neck became very 'wooden', it had no flexibility, it was absolutely stiff, and we went in a straight line, regardless of the ground to be covered. Sporadically, though, he would suddenly slow right up - the engine had been switched off. Nod would shake his head and look about himself, as if saying "Where am I?" or "Oh God, what have I done?" then the fuse would blow again and off we would go, at the speed of a racehorse over anything and everything.

In an attempt to find out why this was happening, Richard the McTimoney chiro-practitioner from Hexham called several times and could find nothing physical to explain Nod's condition. Its roots had to be psychological. In desperation, I rang up the previous owner and asked if he could send up the lad who had hunted him last season.

"Sorry, he has done a flit and gone abroad", I was told.

How convenient I thought.

Nod went out to hounds twenty six times that season, but it would be difficult to describe it as a pleasure. Mostly we were hill topping. This is when hounds and the mounted followers go one way and you on your own go another. You aim for high vantage points from where you are able to see over a large area of the countryside. To be able to do this, you have to know the lie of the land like the back of your hand and to have a very good idea of the likely routes a fox could take. The amount of activity involved in hill topping allowed Nod to be absorbed in what was going on, but withheld from direct action thus preventing the fuse in his brain from blowing. And most important of all, he knew he was needed. Home again, he could tell the other horses what a busy and fun day he'd had. On a few occasions I did field master on him, but by heck that was alarming. This horse was phenomenally fast, powerful and bold, had no self-control and was without the ability to listen to instructions - phew, it was scary! Luckily though, the strain of field mastering was placed on the very competent shoulders of the other three.

Ben you know.

JoJo was an Irish draught grey mare, slightly smaller in height than Nod and Ben, but built like a tank, very strong, able to carry a whole family and their picnic. What a determined lady she was - if she didn't like something, woe betide you if it wasn't instantly put right. Thoroughly self-possessed, she was a real character, a genuine bang-'em, crash-'em and barge-'em merchant as honest as the day she was born. She had not been designed by nature for speed, but she learnt to gallop and could cover the ground with a long stride, which she could maintain for long periods because of her immense stamina. She was a bold jumper - she lived for hunting.

Lucy was a petite 15.2 hand chestnut mare, very fleet of foot, brilliant jumper, exceptionally sure-footed. Once, after a sharper overnight frost than expected, she was two strides out from jumping a gate in the middle of a large puddle and committed to jump, when I realised the puddle was frozen solid. Lucy took off on ice, landed in ice, without a slip and galloped on. She was a dream to field master on. A very neat, affectionate and dainty horse, a pleasure to look after and you always knew that you'd get a 'thank-you' when you did things for her.

The team of horses - Nod, Ben, JoJo and Lucy - all went out to grass for their summer holidays at the end of the season, having notched up a hundred and seventeen days between them. With rugs off, shoes off, they could stretch their toes, roll in the mud, chomp lazily at the grass, yawn, snooze, flick flies off each other with their tails and unwind like free souls. Here they were without human involvement in their lives, a small herd with their own pecking order, routines and self-disciplines.

JoJo

Lucy

Chapter 3

Introduction of Kate Solisti

On the first of July 1994 the team came in, all looked in great shape and the usual procedure to get the horses fit for hunting commenced. On exercise Nod was much improved and he even gave little bucks of happiness as further evidence to his physical progress.

The season started on the first of August, and I entertained high hopes that all was well. But the moment Nod was in action out hunting I could see that there had been no change to his mental condition. My frustration was immense - physically, things had improved, his eating and drinking had returned to normal, his hooves grew so the farrier was able to shoe him easily, he was responding to medicines and radionics. But mentally we were still at square one.

Nod was fed on barley, a more cooling food, rather than oats, but it had no benefit. Lavender and I racked our brains again and again, desperate to discover the key to Nod's problem. We tried all varieties of herbal, homeopathic and Bach flower remedies, but no success.

Then, in October, Lavender suggested that I contact Kate Solisti in Santa Fe USA. Kate is well known as an animal communicator. At this stage of her career she required only a photograph of the animal to enable her to communicate with it, so I sent her a photo of Nod and Ben standing together, with a brief CV describing all his problems, but noting those that had been healed.

I was aware that we as individuals are unable to heal, but can become the catalyst to allow the patient to 'clear their channels', and so heal himself. I was very excited, but also a touch apprehensive - what was Kate going to discover in her conversation with Nod?

I have said to people out hunting "listen to your horse" and can get some funny sideways looks - but I only get a flash of a message. I remember once - I was galloping uphill and my horse was overtaking another, ridden by a lady with all the skill of a sack of spuds. Sitting down on her horse's back. As we passed them, I listened to her horse and distinctly heard it say, "Christ, this bloody women is killing me". I shouted at the woman "stand up in your stirrups, and get off that horse's back". She wasn't amused.

Some girl this Kate Solisti, though. She can apparently have running conversations with horses.

We have to learn again to listen to animals, for we have lost this ancient art. Humans have communicated with all types of creatures for thousands of years and I am eternally grateful that this skill is being re-taught by exceptionally competent people. Monty Roberts, the great Horse Whisperer, has been able to teach the conventional horse world how to communicate with equines through body language. But this is just one of three ways that we can talk with them, as I was to discover.

There is huge interest in all this and the media is now spreading the word. The communication Kate Solisti uses is a form of telepathy and it can take place at a distance; the animal does not need to be present. I suspect that this is how animals communicate with each other as well as vocally. The conversations Kate is able to have are utterly astonishing. She appears to possess the wonderful gift of being able to talk to animals telepathically in just the same way that we humans beings talk to each other verbally - which can be fraught with problems too!

A 'dumb' human like me would require a dictionary and phrase books in French, German, Spanish and Italian just to communicate with my own kind as I ride across Europe. My horse and our travelling companion, a dog, would need no such baggage. Using nature's body language, animals are able to communicate with their own species, and also have the gift to understand us.

We sophisticated humans have to settle for artificial aids, like the fax machine, which is a great communication tool, but can also be a pain in the arse, as I was about to discover. Because of the different time zones between Scotland and Santa Fe, Kate's answer invariably arrived at three in the morning. Woken by the fax, I was always intrigued to read what Nod had to say about life - but then, of course, I had to try to get back to sleep again afterwards, with my brain working in overtime. Kate roared with laughter when, an age later, I told her about this.

Horses are totally honest, they never tell lies. The bad news, she learnt, concerned the way in which Nod had been treated earlier in his career. A previous owner, a very self-absorbed and conceited man, had controlled him by starvation and parching. Nod had not been fed before being taken out hunting, worse still, water had been withdrawn from him the day before; all deliberately designed to weaken him. It is indicative of Nod's phenomenal strength that, physically handicapped as he was, he still managed to hunt. But even giving his all, he was not looked after with respect, never fed and watered correctly. Little wonder he had a chronic eating habit as well as other physical problems.

The good news was how happy Nod felt and what a tremendous help, support and comfort Ben had been. Here was someone to whom he could pour out all his trials and tribulations. He desperately wanted to overcome his problems he told Kate and he wanted me to please be patient with him, as he was trying very hard.

I am no saint myself and at times lose my temper with my horses, including Nod, occasionally clouting them, though never deliberately to hurt them. Of course, then I have to apologise. With Nod I sometimes had to walk away, leave him alone for weeks, apart from routine feeding and watering, to allow my intense frustration to subside. I had to learn to take everything one step at a time. Being by nature an organised person, I expect everything to instantly work tickety-boo, but am well aware that with animals time is irrelevant, and patience, patience, patience is often what's called for. At least Nod knew that he was safe, he would always be fed, watered, kept in snug cosy conditions, even if we never found the root cause of his mental trauma.

This was all Nod would say at this stage. As Kate explained, talking to animals is a bit like peeling off the layers from an onion. After one layer is removed, there is another and yet another, before you eventually arrive at the centre. Was Nod ever going to pluck up courage and reveal all? Was this why he was asking me to be patient? What fantastic story had he to tell?

Whilst it was oh so very frustrating for Lavender and me that we were unable to find the key to unlock Nod, I knew that he found it even more frustrating, not being able to perform as a normal horse. Yet it was essential to go on trying, to go on taking him out hunting, to go on showing him that he was needed and loved.

It seemed rather symbolic that at the end of this season, in the spring of '95 a bantam hen made her nest under Nod's manger, clucking back and forth between his legs without a care in the world, quietly going about her business. As he munched up his breakfast or tea, little flakes of oats would drop like manna from heaven for Mrs Bantam, I saw promise in this small event, growth of new life, but was there light at the end of the tunnel?

Chapter 4

Introduction of TTEAM

During that same spring, when the four horses were out on their annual holiday; Nod must have been feeling particularly well, because there were occasions when he seemed filled with joi de vivre, skipping with all four feet off the ground at the same time, just like a little lamb gambolling. What pleasure it gave me to watch a happy horse playing and frisking.

But they were also worrying times for me. Just before Christmas '94 as Ben and I came into a fence at Cavers Carre I spotted a stone on the landing side. No way could we stop, we were committed to jump. He landed with his near fore slap-bang on the piece of rock, instantly he went lame. I got him home and rang for the vet; who scanned his leg and discovered that he had smashed his check ligament - not just pulverised it, the ingredients that made it up had, to all intents and purposes vaporised; there was nothing left but a black hole. Imagine taking a ligament out of a horse's leg, placing it on a bench and giving it an almighty whack with a mallet - that's what Ben's check ligament looked like. He had to go on twelve week's box rest immediately. But even if Ben had recovered quickly, I would still have needed three fully operational horses to do my job and carry Nod as a passenger.

The horses came in on the first day of July and hunting was to start on the last day of that month. But it was apparent even on Nod's first morning that there was no improvement. He was still programmed as before; walk - flat-out trot - flat-out canter - flat-out gallop - charge. The frustration was enough to make me want to scream.

Back I went to the fax machine for more words of wisdom from Kate Solisti. Nod's reply didn't exactly fill me with confidence. He was very, very happy, he said, but would I please go on being patient with him. He was trying very hard to overcome his problem. He wondered if perhaps I could do something else with him, something other than hunting, something that might generate a breakthrough in his mental problem. Whatever, he begged me to be patient. How much longer? I asked myself. The only reply seemed to be - how long is a piece of string?

So, a less than satisfactory response from Nod - after all, I ride to hunt and hunt to ride. I ride to hunt because, for all man's advance in engineering design and manufacture, no mechanical vehicle can better a horse at crossing the countryside while following hounds and witnessing them individually and collectively hunt the scent trail. I hunt to ride, because there is no pleasure comparable to traversing the British countryside in this way, negotiating land owned by people who have given the hunt right of access. A very close and trusting relationship is forged with, a loving four-legged person, one's horse, who enjoys this happiness. Together, you build a new world of empathy, partnership, harmony and balance with Nature and the animal kingdom.

Whilst I pondered Nod's reply, disaster struck again. On a glorious sunny morning early in September, Ben and I were hunting near Hendersyde. We were galloping gently across a stubble field. Suddenly I felt his near fore sink into a piece of soft ground, and as he pulled his leg up, the check ligament broke again. This second accident meant that he needed further box rest, before going off to spend the winter in a small field below Nottylees with a pony called Kizzy, an interlude he found incredibly boring, but he compensated for this by munching through large quantities of hay. Luckily, the field contained the remains of an old brick limekiln, which formed three structures similar to loose boxes. The shelter these provided came in particularly handy during the two weeks of snow and hard frost we had that winter.

In reply to my latest fax regarding Nod, Kate Solisti suggested I got in touch with a vet in Yorkshire. He and his wife were radionics practitioners and Kate thought they might be able to suggest a fresh approach. As an alternative to me doing something different with Nod as he had suggested. Incidentally in this latest talk with Kate, Nod had asked that, since I had sensitive legs; would it be possible for me to ride him without hands? Whenever I mentioned to anyone Nod's request, they fell about laughing. Ride and control Nod without hands? You can't be serious!

I duly contacted them, explained the background and Nod's current problem and they agreed to treat Nod radionically. As Lavender Dower was on holiday in Portugal with her daughter, I talked this idea over with her assistant, Alison Davy. Naturally Alison was rather apprehensive about two practitioners treating the same patient simultaneously, but I was running out of patience - the sooner this problem was cleared up the better. And so I decided to give this extra treatment a shot. The vet also thought that it might be worth intermittently shocking Nod's brain in an attempt to unblock whatever was stuck there. As before, I posted off a piece of Nod's mane.

Some time later, though, I was forced to ring up this new vet as a matter of urgency. The moment the phone was answered and by his wife, I said.

"Whatever you're doing, stop it right now." I had forgotten that in an effort to assist trust, bonding and communication between Nod and myself, Lavender had placed a piece of my hair alongside Nod's in her instrument. The vet applied his shock treatment to Nod's hair, on his equipment, in an attempt to jar Nod's brain into normal activity. With my and Nod's hairs together on Lavender's machine, some sort of symbiosis seemed to take place, and the shock was transmitted straight into my brain, causing me all manner of grief. The vet's wife replied.

"Yes, we will do that, but the trouble with you is that you are too sensitive." She couldn't have been more wrong. The vet and his wife were unaware of what was on Lavender's equipment.

I had to be patient and take one step at a time. Now I was left with only two great horses JoJo and Lucy. Both, though, were coming to the end of their reigns. I found that, on average, horses could do five seasons with me before they began showing me that the pressure was too much. Then I had to find the right retirement home for them, which was far from easy. First I needed to know if they wished to continue hunting, but under a lighter regime or perform at a different discipline. In other words, I needed to know what's best for them.

Then another fax arrived from Kate Solisti saying that Linda Tellington-Jones, from the USA, was in the UK and she thought that it would be a good idea if I contacted her. Linda Tellington-Jones is an internationally recognised horse expert who created the 'Tellington T Touch', a holistic technique that promotes healing, training and communication with animals. She is also the founder of T.T.E.A.M., the Tellington Jones Equine Awareness Method, a pioneering training approach, which can be applied by horsemen of all levels and which she teaches throughout the United States, Canada, Europe and Australia. When I phoned her, she was just about to be driven to the airport for a flight back home to Santa Fe. However, her UK agent, Kate Prentice, with whom she had been staying, offered to help with my special horse. Linda was in the throes of setting up and training a network of practitioners to cover the UK, which Kate Prentice was going to head up.

Anyway eventually it was arranged that Nod and I would set off on a thousand mile round trip to visit Kate down in Sussex for a weekend, early in November. The Mercedes G-Waggon had been fuelled up, the trailer yoked on, the hay net tied up, water container stashed on board the night before. The dogs and I had an early breakfast, Nod loaded on; we left at 6.00am. The slow part of the trip was from Kelso on the A697 to the A1, just above Morpeth, but this was accomplished when traffic was light. Once we hit the A1, the journey was a doddle, all dual carriageway or motorway, and not a traffic jam in sight. Finally, we whistled round on the M25 and arrived in Sussex by 4.00pm. With all that straight forward driving, no stopping, starting, slowing down, accelerating, constant bends and turns to swing the trailer, Nod arrived relaxed and quite fresh. We had averaged over 40 mph, but then the big 6-cylinder Merc engine pulled well. With such an excellent journey, the angels must have been looking down upon us.

Behind Kate Prentice's very attractive period house and smart garden were some modem timber stables, several fields and an outside all-weather riding school. I unloaded Nod and popped him in a box. I met Kate's horses and dogs, saw that he was settled in all right and went off to a B&B establishment about five miles away.

The next morning, before Kate started to work with Nod, I explained the problems that he had previously had and the outstanding problem still to be solved. I then rode Nod in the school, while Kate watched and analysed his action. After I dismounted, she spent some time doing hand exercises and obedience tests, as laid out in Linda Tellington-Jones' book *Getting in Touch with Horses*. Later in the afternoon, Kate rode Nod for the first time. She soon realised the problem we were up against. Before that, she confessed that she'd been a bit of a doubting Thomas, because Nod and I appeared like a man and horse totally relaxed with each other.

How could Nod have a mental crisis? There couldn't be a problem, surely? Ah, but now she had seen and felt it for herself....Nod's brain simply stops functioning and all you're left with is: charge - bolt.

The next day, Remembrance Sunday, she continued working with Nod on a similar program to the previous day. In the middle of the morning, Sarah Fisher, who currently heads the Tellington-Jones' practitioners in the UK, arrived and they both continued to work with Nod. By late afternoon it was obvious that no dramatic breakthrough had taken place or was going to. The three of us had a discussion on the best move forward. Kate Prentice reckoned that she would need Nod for five days in order to reprogram him. I loaded up Nod for our return journey and travelled that evening to Gloucestershire, to stay with friends and all their four legged companions.

Next morning, we continued our journey, first going to the VWH hunt kennels and picking up three stallion hounds. Before coming south I had constructed a special compartment in the front of the trailer for these foxhounds. Then we went to visit Lavender Dower, who was back from Portugal and her assistant Alison Davy. There Nod showed the ladies what a handsome fellow he was. We travelled on north via the M6, pulling into the Duke of Buccleuch's hunt kennels that evening, everyone happy with the travel arrangements apart from the hounds, poor souls, they had suffered dreadfully from travel sickness. These hounds, after hunting locally, were to be used to father puppies.

We got home eventually, glad to know that we could sleep in our own beds at last. But I was very disappointed and frustrated that no improvement had taken place with Nod. I'm a person who generally expects instant answers and immediate solutions, so having to wait and to progress slowly, step by step with long pauses between, is very galling indeed. However the trip had been worthwhile, as I had learnt about T.T.E.A.M. work and watched two practitioners perform. To curb my feelings I knew that yet again I was going to have to back off Nod for some weeks to let emotions subside. My more serious and immediate problem though was, with Nod not functioning and Ben broken down, I had only Lucy and JoJo to carry the whole load of field mastering - nowhere near enough horses.

Before this trip to Sussex, I had made unsuccessful enquires about the availability of another horse. But now I had to take action. Around this time, I also started to have falls out hunting; these were out of character for me and each fall was progressively harder. Worse still. I had no explanation for these accidents.

Early in December I arranged to go south to Cheshire to look at six horses. I picked out two to try the next day with the Cheshire Forest Hunt. The yard owner suggested a third, as he considered that horse was a good sort. I tried the third horse first, although he was indeed a good horse, he did not have the quality, speed or stamina to cover the country up here in Scotland. I then got on Milly, a six-year old dark bay mare. She was the horse I most preferred, but she decided not to jump fences, not even a tiny one, which of course was no use for my job. But the final horse, Dermot, a 16.3 Irish dark bay gelding, he went well for me in the field, galloped on strongly and flew over fences. Good I thought. I bought him there and then, stopped hunting early, loaded him up in the trailer, and took him home to Scotland that evening.

Chapter 5

Introduction of Morag MacDonald-Worsley

Unfortunately, I soon found out that Dermot was not a front runner. He was very happy, keen and willing to go as number two, but he just died under me when I put him in front; all his enthusiasm and confidence drained out of him. Worse still, he was a woman's horse. By making this bald statement I am not being derogatory to the fair sex. The vast majority of horses do not mind whether they have a male of female jockey, but a few show a distinct preference to one sex over the other. Nod was a man's horse, a bit butch, macho, no sissy stuff- the sort that knows he's a particularly fine male of the species and won't take orders from women. He refused to be fussed over, petted, hugged, or any of this lovey-dovey nonsense - and no way would he allow you to wash his face. Dermot, however, was more effeminate and whilst he tolerated men, his preference was for girls.

During the autumn of 1995, I read a fascinating book on *Feng Shui*. I wanted to extend my knowledge of this subject, so I paid a visit to the Chinese restaurant in Kelso and asked the waiters there how I could learn more. They got quite excited about this and there was much chatter in the back, then they suggested that I contacted "honourable cousin in California". I thought that was just a trifle extreme, but it's funny how fate has other cards up its sleeve.

Because of my uncharacteristic falls while out hunting, I had an appointment with the back specialist in Edinburgh, whose consultation room was in the building occupied by the Holistic Healing Centre. The notice board in the foyer displayed information about a forthcoming seminar on *Feng Shui*, to be given by Mike Robinson, in January 1996 in this centre. I arranged to attend this talk by reserving a place with a lady called Morag McDonald-Worsley, who, unbeknownst to me at the time, was to be the next major player in Nod's saga.

We had two and a half hours of lectures in the morning, followed by the same in the afternoon. When it was over, Morag came across to talk to me and she asked about my horses. She seemed genuinely interested and so we discussed each one in some detail. Eventually, of course, I mentioned Nod, my special fellow, explaining how he still wasn't right after two and a half years.

At this, a strange expression crossed her face, her eyes appeared to go glazed and, in a weird sort of monotone, she said "But you have healed everything in *this life*; you have to heal his *past lives* now."

Well, my brain was buzzing with five hours' worth of lecture on *Feng Shui* and wasn't really in the mood for this sort of nonsense. What on earth was the woman talking about? The aims of *Feng Shui* are to enable men and women to find their ideal living environment and through this, to attain health, prosperity and happiness. It is an art - a science to some of its keenest exponents - that has existed in China for three thousand years. Drawn from the most basic elements of life, *Feng Shui* is the result of the profoundest thought and observation of the relationship between man and nature. What has this got to do with *past lives?* What are *past lives* anyway?

A couple of days later, curiosity got the better of me so I phoned Morag and asked her to repeat exactly what she had said. She apologised, saying that she didn't normally just blurt this sort of thing out, but she had been so overcome with her feelings for Nod as I was talking about him that she was unable to contain herself. She explained that she had been healing horses for over twenty years by treating their past lives and that she "knew" that Nod and I had been together before - in fact, this was our fourth lifetime together.

My reaction was one of total incredulity. I was dimly aware that the Hindus had some sort of reincarnation theory. If you lived a good life, you came back as a higher being - and conversely, if you lived a bad life you returned at the bottom of the pile. Anyway, sceptical as I was, I figured I had nothing to lose by listening to what the woman had to say - in for a penny, in for a pound - and I was prepared to try any avenue in search for the key to unlock Nod. Also I had to admit, I was intrigued. So I made an appointment for Morag to come here and visit us both. What hidden secrets were about to be revealed? I wondered.

Though Nod and I were still going out hunting, I was well aware that I was sitting on a horse whose brain was not working normally and who could be restrained only by the use of intense physical force. While we did no more than walk about watching the hunt from afar, he coped well and was in control of himself. But once I asked him to do anything more, the gramophone needle dropped into a deep grove in the record and simply got stuck there, each time with the same result - charge! It was irrelevant what ground we crossed, what obstacles there might be - ditches, fences, whatever - he'd simply go faster and faster until flat out. As we galloped along I would keep repeating "Think, think" or "Listen, listen" or Take your time, take your time." There were occasions when he would slow right up, when the engine had switched off. Nod would shake his head, look around and you could almost hear him thinking, Where am I? Or Oh God, what have I done? But then the fuse would blow; off he'd charge again. This was unnerving to say the least and I desperately wanted to know why Nod's brain seemed to get stuck like this.

Being blessed with good balance, my falls are rare. The first peculiar one was off a horse called Barny, but it was so insignificant that a casual observer would have assumed for safety reasons I'd deliberately dismounted to prevent an accident been caused by a lorries' tailboard flapping in the wind. Not so - he dropped me. My second fall was off an excellent horse called Monkey. I had placed him correctly at a downhill fence but as he took off, his hind feet slipped from under him, poor fellow. I hit the deck with a bang. The third fall was off Dermot, I had deliberately tucked him behind another horse so he had a lead. On the last stride, instead of taking off, he elected to run out straight through a wire fence. At the Lauderdale hunt ball that evening my face looked as if I had gone a few rounds with Mike Tyson.

As I was scheduled to go south soon for the Waterloo Cup I rang the yard from whence Dermot had come, and explained the problem I had with him not being a front runner. Meantime, this yard had been puzzled by Milly's behaviour with me, in that she had refused to jump when I rode her out hunting. She had won a number of competitions in Ireland before coming to England, so it was difficult to understand. They had the vet out to examine her and a blood test showed up some deficiencies. They put her on a course of treatments with satisfactory results and she was fully recovered. The yard very kindly agreed to swap Dermot for Milly, which I did when I went down for the Waterloo Cup coursing meeting near Aintree.

My fourth fall was off my great horse JoJo. We had met one snowy winter's day at Cotfield, for what turned out to be a very good day's hunting. The first hunt took us across the A7 in a westerly direction, but the depth of the snow was impossible to judge in places, so one couldn't read the ground beneath. Because of this, plenty of horses galloped into snowdrifts, pulling up abruptly with resulting empty saddles - but at least their jockeys usually had soft landings. The last hunt started at Shielswood cattle grid. The first obstacle we met was a simple timber fence of no great height, something that JoJo could jump blindfolded. One stride out though, a considerable force pushed us sideways. There was no sense of wind - nothing to explain it. It was as if an invisible giant had pushed us. Though I tried instantly to correct JoJo's line, we were shoved through a wire fence to the side of the wooden one. I was pitched straight over and JoJo, her legs entangled in wire, crashed down on top of me. I was severely winded and in a lot of pain. It was some time before I recovered enough to remount and when I did so it was against the advice of a friend who'd stayed to help. But by now everyone else had disappeared and I was determined not to miss out. I set off and slowly overtook the back markers. By the time they'd finished I'd caught up, having crossed the Borthwick Water near Roberton at Bitstone Plantation.

Although I was in considerable discomfort, I dined with friends that evening, soon finding myself the source of much amusement. I was unable to coordinate the movement of my right arm and managed to knock over several glasses of port. It turned out that I had broken several ribs and was grounded for some weeks.

The following morning, Morag didn't arrive at the appointed time. A fax came from her friend Sally Spencer, explaining that Morag's car has broken down on the Edinburgh bypass. When we eventually made contact with each other, she apologised for her failure to turn up, but I explained that with broken ribs I wasn't able to get about much anyway, so no hassle.

But what Morag then went onto say threw me completely. It was time, she declared, to deal with the General's spirit. Apparently, he was now so angry that he might cause me an even more serious accident.

What on earth was she going on about? A spirit? A general's spirit? How could a spirit be responsible for these out-of-character falls? How could a spirit push JoJo sideways? Had Morag lost her marbles? Whatever, Morag was convinced that this general's - whoever he was - and Nod's spirits were interlocked, so we agreed to meet the following day. Maybe it wasn't only Morag who had lost her mind - maybe I had too....

Chapter 6

Other complimentary therapies

When Morag met Nod that first time, she began by making the usual comments that all people like to hear about their horse, saying what a handsome fellow he was and so on, putting us both at ease. Then she told me that she wanted to run her hand over Nod's 'energy' field.

Oh yeah, and what was that all about I wondered. She explained that every living creature gives off energy, and if all was well it should appear to her as an exact replica of the physical body, with its external edge positioned about six inches above its surface.

Anyway, Morag did the business, running her hands carefully over Nod, and once she'd finished she announced that he had no energy at all emanating from him in two places: the top of his head and at his hind quarters immediately above his tail. Next, she showed me how to feel this energy for myself. And - surprise, surprise - I *could* feel it. Also, it didn't take me long to realise what she meant - no energy was apparent at either of the two places she'd referred to. The area on top of his head made sense, I knew there were problems there, of course, though no obvious sign of an injury, thank goodness. But the region above his tail was a mystery. Again, there was no sign of damage in that immediate vicinity, but Morag explained that not only did we have to take past lives into consideration, but also be aware that living tissue has its own memory bank. In other words any injury suffered at a particular point in the body has the potential to be 'remembered' by the subsequent tissue if it is unhealed and any adverse effects are retained until such time as the flesh is healed.

What she would have to do now, she said, was trace any accidents in Nod's past lives that may have been left untreated, almost definitely causing his loss of energy.

Ah, so Monty Roberts communicates by body language, Kate Solisti talks to them in their current life by telepathy - and you, Morag, you communicate on a soul-to-soul basis, reading past lives, I see....Well, that shouldn't be too difficult to swallow!

Morag was to have two further visits before the tales were unravelled and when she at last began to describe the events that had occurred in Nod's previous incarnations, I was able to discern something of the substance of the stories. And slowly, very slowly, I became a convert to her way of thinking. Morag's revelations may at first seem like the stuff of fairy tales, but bear with me, please. When you hear what happened, you may begin to think differently.

The first episode she described occurred around five hundred years ago. (I know, I know, but like I said, bear with me.) Back then, Nod had apparently belonged to an Arab, a Bedouin whose tribe, being nomadic, travelled the desert on their horses and camels, carrying and trading goods. Their horses were trained to never lie down - that way they were always ready for instant flight. But there was an exception to this rule. By tapping the near fore, the tribesmen had taught their horses to lie down flat, thus providing a certain amount of shelter if ever bandits raided the Bedouin caravan. In one such raid, Nod was seriously injured when a bullet lodged in his hindquarters just above his tail. This wound went gangrenous and he died.

This story certainly explained why there was no energy at this spot and why he never lay down to sleep. When Morag said that the only way she could get the energy to return to his hindquarters was by releasing the Bedouin's spirit from Nod's spirit, I assumed it meant she was going to carry out some form of exorcism. To this day, I do not know what she actually did, but it worked. From then on, the energy returned to that area and Nod has lain down to sleep. I never did discover the place on his leg where the command to lie down was given.

After Morag had returned to Edinburgh, I gave the dogs a quick turn, pondering on what had transpired that afternoon. And then something struck me - it seemed to zip straight into my brain; the Bedouin in his present-day incarnation was my Father. This was quite fantastic! Was I now able to pick up messages in the same way that Morag could? I went back to the house and phoned her, telling her what I'd worked out.

"Well," she said, "I told you'd been with Nod previously, so the fact that your current earthly father was the Bedouin isn't surprising. Remember what I said about soul groups coming back together?"

According to further 'pictures' that Morag received, the accident responsible for Nod's head injury had occurred when he and I were together.

In that earlier existence, I was a junior officer in a cavalry unit with Nod, my charger. We travelled back and forth throughout Spain, engaged in attempting to outmanoeuvre the French with some skirmishes, then wintering in Portugal. During this time Nod established the reputation for being an exceptionally brave horse. One spring, yet again we broke out of Portugal and this time when we met up with the French a major battle loomed. The general in command of our division had become old and had lost his nerve so was reluctant to charge into battle, though he was still an astute tactician. So, knowing of Nod's repute, he commandeered my horse, hoping to bolster his own courage and led the charge. Regrettably though, a cannon ball blasted off the top of Nod's head.

Ah, so did this explain his wooden neck when he was in charge mode? With tissue having a memory bank, the shock of what happened would have caused his neck to go rigid. Morag stated that the general in question was also the angry spirit that was causing my uncharacteristic falls out hunting. This time, she said, she thought it would be better if I performed the exorcism. She would guide me through the sequence.

I was fascinated by this story, so went off to the big library in Edinburgh to see if I could find any factual evidence. In the shelves of books on the Peninsular Wars, 1809 -1814, I came across one that described a particularly famous battle of Wellington's, which appeared to fit the bill. On the 22nd July 1812, a stunning cavalry charge by the British Heavy Brigade took place at the Battle of Arpiles Height, south east of Salamanca.

When it was time, we stood at the side of Nod in the stables.

Morag asked me, "What can you see?".

To begin with I saw nothing. Then, slowly, very slowly an image appeared in my mind. The scene was initially feint, but gradually it strengthened - a flat, dusty plateau, surrounded by dried-up-looking hills. Lots of soldiers on horseback were milling around on the plateau causing whirling dust storms, but some semblance of order slowly appeared as they lined up in parade formation. Once they had settled into their squadrons, a senior officer arrived on a big, white, flashy horse. He took the salute as the squadrons trotted past. This was the victory parade celebrating their phenomenal success over the French, the senior officer was the general who commandeered Nod. The entire scenario was played out like a silent movie in my mind.

I explained everything to Morag, and she said, "Right, do your best never to judge the general, infact you should never judge what occurred in past lives". She then went on to explain how I was to exorcise the spirit. "In spite of the fact that you were bloody annoyed that the general pinched your horse because he was frightened about going into battle, you must honour him. You must congratulate him on this stunningly successful cavalry victory and then ask him if you could please have back the spirit of your horse Nod. Ask him if, in return, he would please accept the spirit of this magnificent white charger on which he has taken the salute.

This I did by playacting the scene, as suggested by Morag, in my brain and I talked to the general's spirit as if he was standing beside me in the flesh.

After that, I suffered no more out-of-character falls. The general had been angry with me because he was frightened that if Nod was healed he would lose him. In the end, though, the general had received much acclaim and rewards heaped on him as a result of this victory and his career advanced to the highest levels. By swapping the white charger's spirit for Nod's spirit he felt that honours were even.

The energy from the top of Nod's head returned. But unfortunately there was still no improvement out hunting. His neck remained wooden and his brain stayed programmed for charge. I phoned Morag, who told me that she was sorry but she had gone as far as she could. Apparently, I was now going to have to battle it out the rest of the way by myself. So I had obviously not got to the centre of his onion, as Kate Solisti would describe it. How many more twists and turns were there to be, if ever I was to succeed? I decided to ask Nod directly what the problem was, nothing happened. Not immediately, anyway.

Weeks later, though, I was standing next to him and another picture story unfolded in my head. I was a young man in Ancient Rome, very much the man about town. Nod was my number one horse, both for war and for pleasure; just as in this lifetime, he was very powerful, fast and had exceptional stamina. I was due shortly to come into my inheritance, but then a false claimant came out of the blue, with powerful backers and sponsors. He submitted a claim challenging mine.

Eventually the two claims were laid before the Senate in Rome. There were Senators who wished me to be disinherited, so after much deliberation the Senate decided that there was to be a race between us, over thirty-five leagues, equivalent to approximately a hundred miles. We were to pick out our best horse and use a lightweight wicker-hunting chariot. On the appointed day we met at the start and raced for Rome. I drove Nod hard, very hard. I was determined to win. I was not going to be beaten by this lying bastard, who was trying to steal my worldly estate. Of course I won handsomely, much to the chagrin of some. But, horror of horrors, Nod dropped dead after winning the race - he had given everything he had for me.

I apologised to Nod for what I had done back then. His life is and was worth more than worldly wealth. And now I had discovered that Nod had not been overraced in this lifetime, but thousands of years ago - and by me. In my current life I have never pushed a horse beyond its natural capacity, so it would appear that at least I had learnt a lesson. But whilst this was an interesting tale and was the second of our lifetimes together, it was not to solve Nod's behavioural problem. Perhaps, though, I was beginning to develop this gift of sight, or was I?

A few months later, when the horses were on holiday, my workload wound down and I began to detect the first signs of middle age spread, so I booked a private consultation with Mike Robinson. I had discovered that besides being a *Feng Shui* consultant, Mike travelled the world and ran residential courses on Tai Chi, Qi Gong and spiritual healing. I had long been using radionics, then homeopathy, herbal medicines and finally Bach flowers and acupuncture, as complementary to the standard veterinary cures. Now, through meeting Morag and Mike, I was to learn that there was a whole raft more of complimentary therapies that I had not tried, such as Reiki, aromatherapy, colour therapy, Bowen Technique, reflexology and others. This was all a bit overwhelming and confusing. How could I choose which one, or which combination, to help Nod?

In a second consultation with Mike Robinson, I learnt that animals, like humans, are made of body, mind and soul. The great faith of Hinduism teaches about reincarnation. Mike succeeded in convincing me that not merely did this happen, but that humans return as humans, dogs as dogs, horses as horses, which differs from the principle of Hindu teaching. Locked in our subconscious, said Mike, is an amazing computer with a memory bank detailing everything that has ever happened to us. Our brains store not only the memory of our current life events, but also those of all our previous lives, because the soul never dies.

My mind boggled somewhat at this. My memory of events in this lifetime is dreadful, never mind all lifetimes. But then I contacted the Edgar Cayce centre in Co Durham. I read up on Cayce's teachings from books and papers in their library and found that he confirmed this hypothesis. OK, I thought, I'll buy this idea, especially if it is going to help Nod. Perhaps this was what Morag meant when she said that Nod and I had been together for three previous lifetimes.

I had not gone to have past life regressions carried out by Mike, but in the throes of the consultations, he casually mentioned several lifetimes of mine. One indicated that I had been a senior general in charge of a province reporting direct to the Chinese Emperor, another that I had been a High Priest to the Sun God Ra in Egypt, a third as a Rabbi at the time of Jesus Christ. This was pretty staggering, nay unbelievable! I don't know how he did it - I assumed that it must be something to do with a psychic eye. But it did serve to confirm the work that Morag had carried out on Nod, the guidance and instruction she had given me and finally the Roman tale I had found out on my own.

I continued to ponder on these matters, when a casual and out-of-context remark of Morag's sprung back to mind. She had told me how disappointed her mother had been when she had suggested to her as a child that she should take up modelling in clay at school and the suggestion had been met by a flat rejection from Morag. A scene started to form in my mind of large workshops, where sculptors, artists and craftsmen were working away creating a model army. Intrigued, I went off again to the big library in Edinburgh.

Yes, soon it all fell into place now. Zheng became the first Emperor of China in 221 BC. He had the Terra Cotta army built. So, was I a Chinese general of that period, with my horse Nod sculpted by Morag? No wonder she never wanted to do any more sculpting.

Chapter 7

Milly arrives

Milly was a 16.2 hand dark bay mare with a white star and line on her forehead, a seven-eighths bred and she was pretty - and boy, didn't she just know it! Once I'd got her home. I began to learn about her. She was surprisingly 'mareish' when in season, quite coquettish in fact, which one would not have expected from her appearance and it had the disadvantage of affecting her performance. She did like to buck - not serious "I am going to get you off" bucks, but fun bucks and she always gave plenty warning by wiggling her ears before she got started. Much more seriously, though, she reared. She reared both when led and ridden, raising herself upright and teetering on the point of no return, in the most dangerous way imaginable.

Unable to find a reason for Milly's rearing, I phoned Morag. You can probably imagine my surprise when she told me that not only had I been with Nod in previous lives, but also with Milly. Here we go again, I thought - just as well none of this was now new to me.

My prior involvement with Milly, Morag said, was during the Georgian era. Apparently, I had been an immensely wealthy man then, with a big estate and huge investments. I was also a very senior government minister. I had hundreds of horses, with teams kept around the country so I could post chase as required. "And then you gave Milly to your mistress." Morag said.

"I did what?"

"You gave Milly to your mistress. But that's all I am able to tell you, I'm afraid. You'll have to work the rest out for yourself."

I see....

Right, Milly, what is all this rearing about? Looks like I'm off on another mystery tour.

As with Nod's Roman life, I found that the answers were unlikely to come instantly. I had to be patient, waiting for the horse to decide the right moment to spill the beans. Often the answer arrives in the morning and all I can assume is that, when asleep, my soul is free to go off in search of clues. One thing I've definitely discovered is that my brain has to be quite blank, totally clear, uncluttered with thoughts, worries, imagination or ideas. The information arrives in the form of a silent movie - clear, concise and totally incontestable in its simple honesty.

The story was revealed to me several days later. My mistress was the daughter of a portly gnome of a man - a professor. She was very bitter with her father because he would not have her educated when she was a child. But in that era, no girl, no matter how high born, was educated. She was also very annoyed with me. I had a position in high society, immense wealth and was a powerful force in politics - everything she craved and yearned for. The one thing I would not give her was my hand in marriage. I was a bachelor, the girl I loved was a lowly domestic servant and marrying a servant would not have done my standing in the world any good. I was proud of my position in society, especially being nouveau riche. I enjoyed my mistress in bed; she could have, within reason, all the material comforts, but marriage: no. Besides, I knew deep down that she didn't love me truly, just my assets, rank and lifestyle.

In order to force the issue and to create a crisis, she sallied forth in her gig from the house on the country estate where I kept her. She had instructed the groom to deliberately tighten the bearing rein excessively. Sure enough, she caused an accident. When going up an incline with the reins so tight, Milly was unable to pull correctly and came over backwards. My mistress had hoped that by so doing I would be frantically worried about her, to such an extent that I would ask her to marry me. No such luck. I got much pleasure from her body - end of story. Besides I was in a blistering bad temper over the damage she had caused to Milly. It was also revealed to me that my life then was to be cut short.

On the assumption that this recollection was correct, with the trauma still locked in Milly's memory bank, I was going to have to release the bearing reins and unlock my mistress's spirit from Milly's spirit.

I went and stood next to Milly in the stables. I now had to go through a form of play-acting. I visualised the scene in my mind. My mind transcended time and space. I approached the carnage of the accident then and unbuckled and cut the harness and the offending bearing reins. This allowed Milly, who had been grossly over bent, to stretch her neck - all restrictions had been removed. Next, I had to release my mistress's spirit from Milly's spirit, so the play-acting in my mind continued. I called up her spirit and talked to her, just as if we were together in the flesh. I introduced my mistress's spirit to another man's spirit, a man who wished to marry her.

Milly ceased to rear. Now very intrigued, firstly with what Morag had told me, then what I had discovered, and baring in mind that I had proved to myself about Nod's life on the Peninsular Wars, what if anything could I find out to back this tale up? So I was off to the big library in Edinburgh again.

There I came across mention of the South Sea Bubble, a massive speculative financial fraud, which came to a head in 1720. After studying this piece of history, I concluded that back then I had been James Craggs the younger, a government minister who died aged thirty-five.

Years later, I met a girl who triggered one of those flashes of insight in my brain. In the seventeen hundreds, this girl had been my mistress. But not merely that, she had achieved in this life time her worldly burning ambition of being married to a man in the higher echelons of society, loaded with wealth and power. The marriage, however, crumbled and was dissolved; but later she remarried and this man was the spirit I had introduced her to when releasing Milly from her trauma.

My life in the Georgian times was going to crash because of the South Sea Bubble scandal. I would have been forced to resign from the government, retire from society and live a humdrum existence on my country estate. All because of my unwitting involvement with the financial crooks who had thought up this gigantic fraud and I was not in a position to fight back and clear my name.

Morag had told me that soul groups come back together and this made me reconsider some things....

I had recently been swindled by foreign exchange dealers, who were prosecuted by the Securities and Futures Authority Ltd, after the Fraud Squad had raided them. Could they be the same people - reincarnations of those earlier crooks behind the South Sea Bubble? Also, in this lifetime I am a bachelor, who has suffered excruciatingly painful love affairs, the pain so intense and long-lasting that I even considered suicide. Was I being taught a lesson? In that Georgian life I had treated love with contempt - I could buy any pleasure I wanted to. And then there was the servant girl, who eventually bore me a child and who truly loved me, as I truly loved her; but I wouldn't marry her, as she was someone from the lower orders.

I suppose I was paying penance in this lifetime.

But if and when we meet again in the future, oh boy, what a love match we will have.

Karen getting on Nod

Karen on Nod and Gillian on Ben

JoJo in 1996 with me

The Dodger in 1910 with my Grandfather.
JoJo and The Dodger not merely have very similar
bodies but they are the same horse.

Chapter 8

Morris arrives

At the end of that season, JoJo and Lucy went off to their lovely retirement homes and Ben, Nod and Milly went out to grass for their holidays. Some weeks later, in May '96, I called to see Joan, one of my friends in the village and found her sister Hazel was visiting her from the south. Hazel asked if I was looking for another horse and when I replied that I could be, she told me that she had a bay cob, a five-year-old gelding called Morris. He had a lot of problems, though, she said. He napped very badly, refused to go in a trailer - he'd ditched Hazel several times - and suffered from bad angleberries (warts) around his nearside eye, his sheath and between his hind legs. He didn't sound like a suitable replacement for either JoJo or Lucy! Further I could barely believe that a dealer had sold what sounded like a completely unsuitable cob to a woman approaching seventy years of age.

Later, Hazel jumped into my jeep and we drove off to the field where the horses were on holiday. I talked to her about these different characters and asked her how Morris compared to them physically. She explained that he was smaller than any of them, probably nearest in size to Milly.

I was expecting to make a trip south in the near future, so it would be possible to make a large detour and pay Morris a visit. As it turned out though, this trip was cancelled, so I was never able to inspect him physically. Instead, I sat down and contacted him through telepathy. Looking into his soul, I saw that here was a straightforward little character who was waving a flag marked 'Help' to get over some mental problems. Unable to refuse him, I arranged for the local horse transport firm to uplift Morris and fetch him home to Scotland the next time they were way down in the south of England.

When they pulled up that day with Morris on board, the driver told me that he had to get a pony out first before he could get my horse out. So I went round to the stables to collect a headcollar. When I returned to the wagon, the driver was holding a small cob. When was he going to get my horse out? I asked him, thinking I was looking at the pony.

"No, this is your horse," he told me.

I looked again. Flipping heck, Hazel! Your idea of Morris being a little smaller than Milly is way off beam. It was just as well my trip south had been cancelled, because by no stretch of the imagination did Morris measure up to the physical specifications I require in a hunter: he would have been instantly rejected. Here was a small cob, just 15.2, a bright bay gelding, who had come originally from Cornwall, a compact looking little chap, with a big white splash down the front of his face like Nod's and with white legs ending in oversized hooves, these particulars announcing that in his ancestry there was a Clydesdale relation.

Anyway Morris was turned out with the three horses - it was holiday time for him too.

Our puppy show was later than normal in the summer of '96, so the horses didn't come in until the second week of July and the start of hunting was delayed until the 12th of August. I still had the same two sisters helping to exercise the horses as the previous summer, daughters of the farm secretary. They lived in Kelso, so their mum brought them here and went off to the office, leaving them to chatter like magpies in the stables.

Gillian, now aged thirteen, was upgraded from riding JoJo to Ben. How he liked to show off his size and power, strutting his stuff. Karen, nine years old, was upgraded from Lucy to riding Nod. He was chuffed to bits and proud as punch to take this little girl for rides. Wee tot that she was, the soles of Karen's boots just reached to the bottom of the saddle flap, but I fully trusted Nod to look after her while we were out on walking exercise. Although above all else Nod made it obvious that he was a man's horse, he was nonetheless very happy to be looked after by girls and so gentle with this trusting child. On one occasion, though, something did snap and he bolted, galloped through the village and the long way round back to the stables, roughly a couple of miles. Karen naturally clung on, for grim death, till the stables and then dashed off to be comforted by her mum. When I arrived with the other horses and Gillian and was told what had happened, I was in a blistering bad temper with Nod and gave him a fearful thrashing with the flat of my hand. He was very contrite, humble, apologetic and extremely sorry that he had lost control of himself, and concerned that I would not forgive him and trust him again to be allowed to take Karen for rides. Nod had a close relationship with Karen.

I took it in turns, riding or leading Milly or Morris. Now, Milly was very psychic and saw hobgoblins, I'm sure - and in Scotland hobgoblins are simply enormous compared to the ones back home in Ireland: fifty percent bigger, just gigantic. The moment she spotted one, the anchors would go on instantly. Emergency stop.

"What? Can't you see it?" her expression said, "It's there in the middle of the gateway. There's absolutely no way I can go through the open gate - can't you see? He has got a Viking's helmet on and carrying that big spear - can't you see?"

Morris, however, saw the little people, the elves, pixies and fairies, along with the particularly fierce ones - the little green men - and they have horns. They jump out of their hiding places and by twiddling their ears with their fingers stick their tongues out at him. No way can you go past them. The girls thought this was hilarious.

The worst experience he had was one morning, when I was on my own and I had ridden him down from Windywalls, nearly to Mellendean. There on the side of the track, just before the cottages, was the trunk of an old dead oak tree, that had fallen down in a gale, about six-foot long by two-foot diameter. Well, perhaps it would have been all right if just one little green man had popped up, but no sooner had that first one disappeared behind the trunk than another popped up, then another and yet another, popping up and down in sequence, like targets on a fairground rifle range. Finally they all popped up together and that finished it as far as Morris was concerned. Until then, he had been rooted to the ground, snorting like furry, but no self-respecting horse was going to put up with that sort of behaviour. So he got it into his head to begin spinning like a top, burreling round clockwise then anticlockwise, by which time all the wee green men had ducked down and luckily, we had spun past the trunk.

After a few weeks it became apparent that Morris was paranoid about flies. He became virtually unrideable, shaking and tossing his head, spinning round, rearing up and striking out at them with his front feet. So I asked him what the problem was. The answer came back that the trauma was the result of suffering in two past lives.

Now, whatever you may think of this concept - unbelievable, whatever- astounding, all I can tell you is that I had been convinced after reading about Edgar Cayce, then witnessing both Mike Robinson and Morag MacDonald-Worsley achieving instant communication with past lives. And lately, through their guidance, I had tentatively begun to accomplish something similar. We are all able to walk and run, but some are better at it than others. We all use the five senses of sight, sound, smell, taste and touch, but in these so-called civilised times most of us have lost the sixth sense; our psychic sense. Luckily, more and more people are now activating this sense, cleaning the third eye, in these times of increased spiritual awareness.

Whenever I come across a problem in life, my automatic reaction is, "Oh, how can I help?" The lovely thing about working with animals is that they always want to be healed, so often you *can* help, whereas deep down some humans often don't, even if they pretend that they do. You can talk to horses in exactly the same way that you talk to humans beings and, like all other animals, they always tell you the truth in fact they are incapable of understanding why humans are deceitful and duplicitous.

The few pictures of Morris's first lifetime that I was shown, when he encountered big trouble with flies, were of scenes perhaps a thousand years ago. He was a wild horse grazing peacefully with his herd in an area that looked like the Russian Steppes. Suddenly, some sort of alarm was raised and a few men deliberately set the herd off in panic. Morris charged blindly over a cliff, with a few others from the herd, and crashed to the ground hundreds of feet below. There he lay with broken legs and a smashed body. The flies soon found him and the dead horses, attracted by the smell of fresh blood. They laid their eggs on him and the maggots ate him to death.

Morris's second traumatic experience was probably only fifty years ago. He was a pony living on a massive refuse tip in South America, where he scavenged alongside humans for food amongst the rubbish. Eventually, through poor nourishment and disease, he collapsed and gave up the will to live. The flies descended - the end result, the same.

First I tried just earmuffs, to cut out the sound of their buzz - no improvement. Then I tried the earmuffs with a veil visor - no improvement. So in addition to these bits of equipment fitted to his head, I put Vic up his nostrils and rubbed it over his muzzle - no improvement. Finally, on top of all the mechanical aids, I threw an 'energy blanket' over him while riding him. Success! Morag had taught me to feel energy coming off horses, so as I was riding along, I deliberately expanded my energy and allowed it to flow over Morris's, in the same way that you would throw a huge blanket over a horse, thus enveloping him. I also started to treat his angleberries with Thuja cream but he was such a fusspot about this that he was put on radionics to get them under control. There was no way a vet could have operated on the ones by his left eye.

Now I had to do something about his refusal to go in a trailer. Wagons were OK but trailers no. The trailer was yoked onto the jeep, front and rear ramps down, breast bar swung out of the way: let the fun commence!

Morris now showed me a piece of his character previously hidden.

"What a very determined, obstinate little chap I am," he said. He stood there with all four feet planted firmly on the ground. With the Clydesdale in his breeding, Morris's hooves were the size of small dinner plates and they might just as well have been glued, stapled and nailed to the ground as far as my chances of moving him were concerned. The expression on his face, "If you think I am going in that trailer you can just think again, because I'm not - and that's my last word on the subject". I think someone once said you can lead a horse to water but you can't make him drink. That was the situation I was in.

"Morris," I told him, "you are going in that trailer."

"Oh no, I'm not."

"You are."

"Not!"

"Oh yes you bloody well are!"

Did we have fun! It kept someone in an office amused watching the antics; you can picture it - no matter what some pundits say, you cannot force a horse to do something against his will. This battle of wills went on for some time. At a pause in the conflict, as both combatants had run out of puff, I asked Morris, "OK, so what's all this nonsense about?"

To my surprise I received an instant response. Before then, any replies from my horses had taken days, if not weeks.

But the lifetime Morris was about to divulge to me showed me something altogether new about him. His cast-iron will had sadly played a major part in his downfall.

I think this was about the eighteen-seventies to eighteen-nineties and in an area on the Mexico - USA border. Morris was a wild horse, running with his herd, when they were captured by cowboys. Now normally of course, cowboys or stock-handlers are professionals, good at their job. They handle animals with experience and understanding. These cowboys, however, were not simply bad at it, they were cruel. Having captured this herd of mustangs, they set about breaking them and I mean *breaking* I am not using the word in its incorrect modern meaning of training a raw horse to be ridden.

Anyway the cowboys managed to break all the captured mustangs, bar Morris. He stood his ground, he fought them and fought them and fought them; no way was he going to give in to them. They were livid. Time was running out and they wanted to cash in the haul of horses they had broken. They were furious that this one horse still totally defied them and that they could neither ride nor mount him. So they decided that the only thing to do was to take him to the meat factory.

They roped him up and tied his legs tight up to his belly. Monty Roberts has pictures in his book of this extremely cruel way of roping and tying up a horse, just like his own half Cherokee/European father used to do. Here was Morris, a bundle of live horse-flesh, parcelled up with only his neck and head able to move. Then, to torture him, they did the cruellest thing imaginable; they took a mug of water and poured it down one of his ears. They did this in a fit of pique and blind rage. Sometimes they would use lead shot instead of water. If your horse, for whatever reason, gets totally bogged and exhausted this can, very rarely, be the correct thing to do; otherwise it should never be done. By pouring water into his ear you give a horse an amazing energy boost that results in him developing a supercharged strength. Just imagine the pain of having an immense, surging thrust of power coursing through you and yet being totally immobile, unable to release it.

Eventually I did get Morris to walk into the trailer - and straight out the front. Eureka. Finally though - hallelujah! - He walked in and stayed there. Whew! We had both lost pounds in weight. Then I shut the rear and front ramps. He stood perfectly still. All was set.

My next task was to go into a sort of playacting mode that I have mentioned before, whereby I uncluttered my mind, turning it into a blank canvas. Then I visualise a picture of a horse completely trussed up with ropes all over him, unable to move apart from his head and neck. Lifted onto a horse-drawn wagon, this poor creature has become nothing more than a lump of captive live horsemeat. Through the power of thought, Morris and I were enacting the same scene. Mentally, thinking hard, I cut away all the ropes that were binding him tight. I literally cut, untied and removed the ropes from his spiritual body.

One morning towards the end of August, I set off to go hunting with Morris west of Selkirk at Hartwoodmyres. After we had finished, I loaded up again and moved to where the Eton Beagles were going to meet at Mainside and hunt in the nearby Cheviots that afternoon. Morris and I rode to the summit of a grass hill, where the grass gave way to heather in bloom at the very top. From there we had a splendid panoramic view and were able to see for miles along the valley, all the way south to the English border. Way off in the distance, I spotted three cars driving up the track to the old reservoir, the occupants had probably decided to have a picnic there after their day's grouse shooting in the Lammermuirs had been cancelled.

Then the beagles found a hare near the river. Hare and the pack crossed the water onto the opposite side of the valley to me, where the grass gave way to heather much lower down. Morris and I had a grandstand view of this unsuccessful hunt and also witnessed two and a half couple of naughty beagles change quarry and hunt a roe deer followed by fit young whipper-ins running through knee high heather hard for the English border.

Just as we reached the steading (farmyard) at the end of the day, a violent thunderstorm broke out and for five minutes a hailstorm lashed the trailer, so severe I was unable to get out of the jeep. Then came six to seven minutes of solid water, an absolute downpour, like a whole reservoir had been emptied on top of us. The steading was flooded five to six inches deep, the drains unable to cope. Once the storm had moved on I went to get Morris out, but he was having none of it. Our conversation went something like this:

"No," he told me, "I am not for doing that."

"Morris, what is all this about? Once upon a time you wouldn't load, now you refuse to unload."

"I am not going to unload."

"Why?"

"Well, you see, when those cruel cowboys set off for the meat factory with the captured mustangs and me loaded on the trailer, we had a four day journey ahead of us."

"All right, what has that got to do with you not coming out of the trailer?"

"You understand, I was totally tied up, couldn't move and wasn't given any food or water."

"Morris, I know that is a completely unacceptable way to treat any horse, particularly such a brave little man as you, but what has that got to do with not coming out of the trailer?"

"OK, I'll explain. In the middle of the journey, we experienced a violent thunderstorm, like the one we have just had."

"Ah, so this storm, has brought back the memory of those dreadful days."

"Yes."

I went into the trailer and worked on the energy field around Morris's head and then on his head itself with my hands; this process allowed him to release the memory of his appalling trauma, an aspect of his personality that was totally irrelevant to his current life. At length, Morris finally walked out of the trailer willingly and I've had no further problem loading or unloading him since.

Now that he has recovered, we do however have a little game, he never loads straight away and will wait for a second or two at the bottom of the ramp, sometimes even for a minute, until he is good and ready. Then he walks in and we're set to go. This, of course, is Morris gently reminding me that you can't force a horse to do something that he doesn't want to do!

Morris had one other peculiarity though. Whenever he was under the slightest stress from work, or if he was apprehensive about something, a patch of sweat would appear just above his off-side shoulder. The rest of his body would be dry, except for this single two-by-four inch area. Sometimes, if he was doing a little more work than usual, the sweat would virtually stream down his shoulder and leg, but still the rest of his body remained dry. It was as if I had taken a jug of water and poured it on that one patch. I had him checked out for a trapped nerve; nothing showed up via radionics or anything else. At this time Morris was in the box later occupied by Cats. The mystery was eventually solved through another remarkable occurrence one evening when I went to check on the horses.

Looking over the door into his box, I was astonished to find Morris standing there with a spear sticking out of him at the exact spot where this extraordinary sweat patch appeared. The scene he then proceeded to reveal to me was of a lifetime perhaps four and a half thousand years ago, in a part of the world where snow lay thick on the ground and the only trees appeared to be silver birch, but plenty of them. Maybe northern Russia. Morris was a wild horse back then and had been hunted down and captured for food by a skilled hunter.

My next task was evident - I should call up the spirit of that hunter. So I did this and dutifully he came and stood by my side, dressed in clothes made from animal skins. I asked him if he could please pull out his spear and release Morris to me. The hunter was reluctant at first, explaining that he had killed the horse so that he could feed his family and the clan.

"OK, I understand your dilemma," I told him, "but rest assured that I will replace Morris with alternative food."

Eventually, the hunter seemed convinced that I wouldn't let him starve and agreed to remove the spear. He pulled, he tugged, he heaved but the spear stayed firmly embedded in Morris. So I decided to give him a hand by grabbing hold of the weapon and we heaved and wrenched and swore, until finally, with a sudden jerk, the spear came out. Together we fell against the wooden side of the box, four foot away. I gathered some spiders's webs from a corner of the box and laid these over the wound created by the spear - these would stop the bleeding and act as a poultice. As the hunter had now kindly given me Morris, I in return gave him two fat lambs in compensation, thus allowing him to feed his family. I had honoured my agreement with the hunter.

When I checked on Morris a few hours later, I was surprised to find the hunter still there. He was licking his lips and wiping the grease from his mouth with the back of his hand.

"What were those tasteless things I have just eaten?" he asked me.

Damned fool that I am, I'd overlooked the fact that there were no such animals as fat lambs in his era; there weren't even domesticated animals. So I whistled up the spirits of two of my lurchers: Rambo and his hunting partner Bizzy. The four of us went off hunting and my dogs successfully each caught and killed a small roe deer. The hunter was well pleased when I presented him with the two deer in lieu of Morris.

The small patch on the top of Morris's shoulder never reappeared.

Considering all the problems this wonderful little fellow had to begin with, it seemed a disgrace to me that a dealer had sold Morris to a lady approaching three score and ten. But in the end, Morris became a star, an outstanding character- absolutely genuine I-am-what-I-am type horse. He was never anything smart or grand, simply one hundred percent honest and so reliable that I could put anyone on him. He taught children to ride, he was superb when furnishing them with the unmissable experience of their first day's hunting, and he had become a really perky horse that always looked on the bright side of life.

And perhaps the most incredible thing of all was that, once you were sitting astride him, he gave you the feeling that you were on a much larger horse.

Morris, Milly, Nod and Ben setting off on exercise

Chapter 9

Nod visits TTEAM farm and the seaside

Summer 1996: the children had gone back to school at the end of August, so it was time for me to review the situation. Ben was in fine fettle, displaying exactly how powerful he was when on exercise with Gillian. But Milly was temperamental and moody, one day performing very well and the next proving how difficult and volatile she could be. When I discussed this Jekyll and Hyde behaviour with Morag, she once again taught me something new.

"You must remember," she said, "in two of your past lives, the Roman and the Peninsular ones, Nod was your top horse and Milly served as nothing more than a replacement. What you're witnessing now is an inferiority complex - she's intensely jealous of playing second fiddle." I thought only humans had such emotions, now apparently so do horses.

By complete contrast, Morris was a straightforward little character, with a big heart, who, having been debugged, had realised that hunting was belting good fun. Because of his behavioural problems, he had not originally been a natural herd leader, but he had quickly cottoned on to the fact that he carried some importance, since other horses gave way to him. He single-mindedly took up the challenge of leading the field and his determination meant that he was not going to let the side down. On top of that, it was obvious he enjoyed it. Whoopee!

Alas, there was still no improvement to Nod's performance on the hunting field. I had not yet found the centre of his onion, despite three years of trying, searching, seeking help and guidance. If only I could find the code to decipher the jumbled messages in his brain. Then I remembered the request he had made when talking with Kate Solisti. He'd asked me to try doing something quite different with him, to see if this would allow release from his condition.

Luckily, Tellington-Jones T Team (UK) had now set up a base near Redditch, just south of Birmingham at the appropriately named Tack Farm. This was much easier for me to get to than deepest Sussex. Virginia ran the yard and Kate Prentice, a senior practitioner, came up from Sussex on a weekly basis. I arranged for Nod to go south in the middle of September for four weeks. The trailer was yoked onto the jeep and aboard went his luggage of stable rugs, New Zealand rug, his tack - his personal reactor panel saddle, which had been measured and fitted for him, plus the special Tellington-Jones bit on his bridle - hay net and water container. Last but not least, his large pink rock, a present from Morag, a healing crystal. We had a doddle of a journey south on the M6. Would this trip crack his mental blockage?

A few days before taking Nod south, though, disaster struck for the third time. I was hunting with Ben on a beautiful morning on the hills above Hartwoodmyres. The skylarks were trilling above, the odd grouse was indignantly demanding *go back, go back*, and the heather was in full bloom - what more could man want? This was as near to heaven as it was possible to get. The previous day Ben had been clipped and shampooed, and now looked a picture of good health - with coat shining, he was on top of the world. We were gently cruising at a sedate gallop, with Ben as normal watching hounds and not where he was putting his feet. His near fore dropped into a tiny ditch, with a bit of a lurch, he corrected himself. But - *crack* - he was dead lame. The repaired check ligament had failed again and was obviously never going to be up to much. We slowly made our way back to the trailer and on the way I asked Ben what I should do.

"Do I find a quiet retirement home for you," I suggested, "where you would have a little gentle walkabout hacking?"

The instant and unequivicable reply was, "No."

Ben tolerated about ten days of routine exercise to get fit for hunting, but quickly made it very clear that all this slow walking and trotting was incredibly boring, totally unnecessary and not his style. The only thing he was interested in was hunting, as he couldn't do that any longer, Ben let me know that he wished to move on. The next day I took him up to the kennels, where he was put down, with the sound of his beloved hounds in his ears and more tears from me.

Nod had a great time at Tack Farm. Imagine the joy and wonder for someone, who loves fast, exhilarating cars, would experience, if they were suddenly lent an Aston Martin and told, off you go on an all expenses paid four week touring holiday on the continent. Wow! Wow! Well, Nod showed off to the girls something rotten. They did not dare ride him outside of the outdoor riding school, but in it he could demonstrate just what a powerful fellow he was. His fabulous paces, amazing extended trot, dressage performance - they were a piece of cake with all the military training he'd had in his past lives. He exuded power, displayed a grace and aura that announced "I am supreme." Naturally bold, he would jump anything. Yet he was so kind and gentle, a real pleasure to look after and so appreciative of what one did for him. Always interested in what was going on, it was difficult to understand how he still had this major problem with his brain leaving him unable to work in the big wide open world.

I rang Tack Farm near the end of Nod's stay, leaving a message on their answer phone, to confirm when I was coming down and to tell them that on the following day, a Friday, I'd be taking him hunting with the Warwickshire. Well, that seemed to put the cat amongst the pigeons. A few hours later, Virginia was on the phone.

"Oh, you can't do that," she said, "Kate and I have had long discussions, wracking our brains as to what would be best for Nod."

Patiently, I explained, "Virginia, I told you when I brought Nod south that it didn't matter if you weren't able to reprogram him - this exercise was simply to comply with his request that I do something different with him. Of course, I desperately hoped it would be successful, too."

"Ah, but listen.... You see, we found Nod a fantastic horse to ride - his amazing power, comfortable stride through his paces, his phenomenal extended trot - we think he should have a career change."

"What do you mean by that?"

"We think that he should go and perform at dressage, with the occasional shot at a cross country course, where he can gallop flat out."

"But Virginia, that would mean me releasing Nod, selling him, losing control of his destiny. And even if I was to do that, it's inevitable that any new owner would become frustrated with Nod's problem, then he would be sold on and would quickly go down that formidable slippery slope."

"No, I can't let that happen to him again. Nod knows that he's safe in a permanent, loving home. He can never be put through the hell he has had to endure. Besides, Virginia, I have this feeling deep deep down that Nod was sent to me. It's my duty to honour my debts of gratitude to Nod for everything he has done for me over our lifetimes together. If I'm unable to heal him, *so be it*, I will never release Nod."

I set off south with an empty trailer behind the jeep, to collect Nod. While I was driving along the M6 he suddenly sprang into my mind with a request. Could he please go swimming in the sea?

OK, I told him.

I mean right in, not paddling, right in.

OK, I will fix that up when we get home, we'll go down to Spittal Beach near Berwick-upon-Tweed, when the tides are favourable.

I stayed the night with my adopted English family, the Alldays, in Worcestershire. The next morning, Friday 11th August, I collected Nod from Tack Farm.

He did look well, and we went to the Warwickshire Hunt meet at Lighthorne. After hounds moved off, I found that Virginia and Kate were correct, he was still programmed in the old way - ***Charge!*** However, because of the lie of the land and all the good vantage points, we were able to hilltop very successfully and we both thoroughly enjoyed ourselves. Foxes were popping up all over the place - in fact I think there were more foxes than hounds.

When we got home, I found out when was the best time to go to the seaside with Nod and off we went to Spittal Beach, one lovely sunny October day. I took a change of clothes with me and Nod had on an old felt saddle and an exercise bridle. Low tide was at 1.00pm. The sea looked as smooth as a millpond when we arrived, so perfectly still. There was not even the smallest wave breaking on the sandy beach, just the barest ripple the height of a pencil lying on its side, and I could see we are going to have to go a long way out before it was deep enough for Nod to swim. I inspected the beach and thought it looked solid enough for me to drive onto, so I steered down the ramp off the road, travelled fifteen yards and became bogged down. Bugger! Halfway between the sea and me was a courting couple, obviously wondering who on earth this nutter was. I got out, unloaded Nod, tied him up to some rails and unyoked the trailer. Then I drove to the top of the ramps, and fixing ropes to the back of the trailer, hauled it up onto the road. Curiosity had now overcome the couple so they came up to enquire about events. I explained that Nod wished to swim in the sea and I proposed to ride him into it.

Nods rock
measuring approx 24cm wide by 14cm tall

The couple both worked in London and were in Berwick for a holiday. The girl, originally from Dumfriesshire, had ridden as a child. They chatted to the dogs and to Nod. I explained about Nod's problem and that this escapade was the latest in a long line of ventures attempting to find the key to unlock his brain from being programmed to charge. Then I climbed on board and set off for the sea.

Midway between the ramps and the sea was a narrow strip of dark sand, about four foot wide. Nod went spare, completely doolally - under no circumstances was he going to cross that strip. It took me some minutes to realise that he meant it and I couldn't help wondering at his quite extraordinary behaviour. So I went another way around and arrived at the edge of the sea.

Nod refused to go in. Most peculiar. It was dead calm, no waves at all, just tiny ripples gently lapping onto the sand. These ripples wouldn't even cover Nod's shoes, yet there was no way he would take another step forwards. It was a point blank refusal. How astonishing! What was Nod trying to tell me? First he wants to swim, so we come all this way - and he refuses. He wouldn't even cross a strip of damp sand. What could it possibly mean?

We stood there facing the sea and as tiny ripples slowly crept in, Nod backed furiously away from them, terrified. Why? I didn't understand. Nod would plunge into a boiling, raging river in full spate without batting an eyelid. I tried different places along the shoreline with the same result. No way was he going into the sea. I tried to get him to walk into some of the shallow puddles, but he wouldn't have that either. This was so contrary to his behaviour at home - puddles, burns, rivers he'd cross them all without thinking. What on earth was going on in that head of his?

I went back to the trailer, utterly confused. The young couple had been watching all this. When they asked me why he wouldn't go in for his swim, all I could tell them was that I didn't have a clue and that I'd just have to wait and see what he tells me. Then I asked the pretty blonde girl if she would like to have a ride on Nod. She thought that would be brilliant. So she mounted up and set off along Spittal Beach, putting Nod gently through his paces of walk, trot and canter. She was quite ecstatic when she returned and told me this was going to make her holiday. I had a hunch that something else was going to make their holiday - Nod was merely the catalyst to the confirmation of their loving relationship.

I puzzled over Nod's behaviour as I drove him home. Had I misunderstood him about wanting to swim in the sea? Why did he behave abnormally? In a flash he started to answer. He told me about a lifetime, apparently way, way before we were together in ancient China. He was a wild horse and his herd had been grazing along the foreshore of a brackish tidal lagoon. Nod got stuck in some quicksand. The tide turned and the sea slowly and gently edged back into the lagoon. Nod screamed and whinnied at the herd, but they could not help him, they moved away. The sea slowly swept over him and drowned him.

My reaction was, "OK, I understand that and I'm desperately sorry about that dreadful death you had then. It explains why you wouldn't cross the damp sand nor go into the sea - but why did you ask me to take you there in the first place?"

As I waited for Nod's answer, I realised this tale of an horrific death was the last layer of the onion surrounding the centre. Nod was now able to tell all, this terrible confession that had been stuck in his brain for an age. This was the key Lavender, Morag, Kate Solisti and I had been praying and searching for, for three and a half years.

Nod now went back to the story in the Peninsular Wars and enlarged on the story he had originally told when Morag was teaching me about spiritual healing. He had also previously mentioned four other lives as a war horse and no doubt there were many more.

"You see," he explained, "in that charge, when I had to carry that frightened general, my nerve broke and my spirit was shattered. I had never been frightened and terrified in any of my lives as a war horse. I galloped blindly at the French, screaming in fear, then the cannon ball blew the top of my head off."

"Ah, at last I understand. At the moment your brain was destroyed, all the messages and memories locked inside it amounted to one command: Charge in Terror. Charge in Blind Panic."

"Yes, but you see, I was the Supreme War Horse - and I had been broken."

What a gigantic confession.

So that was it! At long last I had got to the core of Nod. Wonderful, pure magic. And now that he was finally able to confess the whole truth of this terrible event, it was now irrelevant to him, for now and for the future. He was able to completely erase the consequences of it from his memory, and his brain was going to be able to function like that of any normal, healthy, happy, loving and loved horse.

The channel was now clear.

I sent Lavender and Morag a bottle of champagne each with the good news and Kate Solisti, courtesy of Interflora, was bunched, as well as receiving a very upbeat fax from me.

Chapter 10

Milly's problems

Milly continued to be stubbornly mareish and I knew she was hiding things from me. She just wouldn't come clean and it seemed I'd not earned her trust or given her any reason to feel comfortable with confiding in me. While working with Nod I always knew that he was trying his best to recover. Not so with Milly; she was so 'hodden doune' with her problems and with the trails and tribulations of her soul group, that she was never able to see the brighter side of life. She couldn't cope - she wasn't even going to try: she just blanked everything off. I rang Morag and we talked about her condition.

Morag was able to pick up a past life, a time when Milly had been a mare living on a small farm, probably on the Cornish peninsula at the turn of the nineteen hundreds. She had totally trusted the farmer and his wife but, after a difficult foaling, they removed her foal. A terrible emotion swept through her - the grief of being unable to mother her child. To compound this tragedy, they didn't look after the foal at all well in her eyes.

Once I understood all this, Milly, who had previously been totally silent, at last started to whinnie for the first time ever. But no, this still hadn't solved the problem. I had more delving to do to find the centre of Milly's onion. The vet suggested she was put on a course of Regumate, but that had no effect. At times a black rage would come over her and she would blindly smash head-collars, stall ropes - anything that represented restraint. Rage is an emotion we do not often meet in horses, so I was at a loss to understand it.

One morning when I went to the stables to give them their breakfast, I found that she had broken the stall rope and then savagely attacked Nod - really laid into him. There had been a few previous occasions when she had bitten Nod on the neck, out of jealousy, but nothing like this barbaric assault on his hindquarters and hind legs, lacerated ugly open wounds. Standing in his stall, he couldn't get away from her, yet he didn't retaliate by kicking out at her. Nod simply absorbed her black rage.

When there had been previous small attacks by Milly on Nod, I had taken her out and put her in the hay shed next door, there being room at the front now that some had been consumed. She did not like being sent to Coventry. The difference this time, Milly, I told her is you stay there until such time as you tell me what this is all about. Silence, one big sulk.

That evening when I checked the horses Milly complained to me, "I don't like it in here."

"Milly, you are bloody well staying there until you cough up what this is all about," I told her.

Anyway, I rang Morag again and as sometimes happens, she was able to start unravelling the problem. Whenever she reached any of the more gruesome aspects, she faltered nature protected her, but I was able to see deeper and complete the tale.

This time Morag was able to pick up a life of Milly's in ancient Egypt. She was the matriarchal mare of a special herd of horses, specifically bred by the Pharaoh for stamina and speed. They were used for pulling light, flexible chariots when out hunting with trained cheetahs, as well as improving the performance in battle of the chariots carrying warriors.

Now, I wondered, could this be a lifetime of mine that Mike Robinson referred to, when I was a high priest to the Sun God Ra? Off to the big library in Edinburgh again. There I found that Ramesses the 2nd was the Pharaoh, who had deliberately undertaken an extensive horse breeding improvement scheme. Also, in Catherine Rommelaere's book *Les Chevaux du Nouvel Empire l'Egyptien Origines, Races, Haratchement*, she mentions tablets of that period written in old Iraqi, which refer to a special Mare. Could that mare be Milly?

The unfolding scenes that Milly showed me were of a conquering army from Syria and Iraq that had defeated the Pharaoh's army in a battle, the troops then set out on an orgy of old-fashioned rape, pillage and looting. They decided to desecrate one of the Pharaoh's highly prized possessions, taking his special herd of horses and tying them to stakes driven into the ground in the middle of a large training amphitheatre. They then brought in the cages containing cheetahs, leopards, and lions and released the big cats on the captive horses. The terror that was inflicted on the horses was horrendous - blood, skin and bone everywhere, total carnage. The warriors then took up their spears and went into the arena and killed the cats and any surviving horses.

The next evening, I went to check the horses for hay and water. On looking into the hay shed, I discovered that there, sitting on the bales behind Milly were some warriors in uniform, looking down at her. They were very sullen, contrite and ashamed of what they had done in their victory celebrations.

Remembering what Morag had said- "Do not judge past actions." I didn't pass comment. Instead I talked with them, honoured these brave soldiers who had defeated the Pharaoh's troops that day and released their spirits from Milly.

Milly lost her black rage.

Milly continued, however, to be contrary. Though there was an improvement in her performance, she could be unreliable over jumping. She could be flying over fences without a care in the world and then, without warning, decide that was enough. I was aware that some of this came from Milly's wish to protect her prettiness, but there had to be an underlying reason, so I asked her what the problem was.

Her answer related to a life when we had been together. It would appear that this lifetime was the one immediately preceding the one when I was fabulously wealthy and powerful in the Georgian times. This is the tale that Milly told me.

In that life I was a penniless public coach driver in the Derbyshire area. A cocky little sod, always skint, I was very pleased with myself that I had a certain reputation for speed, forever pushing my team of horses very hard. One day I pushed too hard going down a steep hill and lost control. The leader of the team- Milly - crashed through a fence on a bend and smashed into the rock face on the other side. The coach was a write-off, and Milly was seriously injured. I was sacked on the spot.

After Milly told me this story there was no improvement in her performance, so I asked her what relevance this story had.

"Swings and roundabouts" she replied. "That's all. Just to remind you about swings and roundabouts. A life of luxury and plenty will be balanced by another life that's quite the opposite."

"Well, thank you for that profound hypothesis," I replied.

Milly continued to be contrary. So again I contacted Morag. "The raven is flying over her," she told me.

What on earth did that mean?

"I told you previously," she went on "that Milly is the soul leader of her group of horses. Nod does not belong to that group, as he is a supreme spirit in his own right, although the three of you are connected. Not only has Milly suffered terrible dramas in her personal past lives, but also her soul group of horses have taken the most fearful hammering and pounding. They off-load their problems onto Milly, the combined load is too great for her."

"Are you telling me that as well as Milly's jealousy over Nod because he was always my number one, she lacks self-confidence? That she finds it difficult to accept affection and love, because she is so 'hodden doune' with her problems and the immense burden placed on her by the horses she is connected with through their souls?"

"Yes."

"So Milly came back to me in this life for help to lift her burden and assist in her healing - help from me and Nod and the matriarchal mare JoJo, both being supreme spirits?"

"Yes."

I understood then that, in a different way, it was a little similar to the deep, deep inner feeling I had that Nod was sent to me. That it was my bounden duty, as then unexplained, to do everything and anything to help him, no matter if I never succeeded. I had an overwhelming obligation to repay Nod for everything he had done for me, and that the same applied to Milly.

Chapter 11

Nod release from his trauma

When I rode around at home Nod appeared fine, physically and mentally in great condition, with his self-control fully functional. The test would come when we were out hunting. I had two consecutive Mondays lined up to take him. The first when I was not on duty, so I would be able to hilltop, going off on my own if necessary. But this time instead of just sticking to vantage points and moving mainly at the walk, I hoped to be able to gallop and jump fences and follow hounds closely. Get really involved rather than being a distant spectator.

That day arrived. The meet was at friends Willem and Jenny Stewart's farm, Springhall, on the opposite side of the Tweed to home. It was a thrilling ride. I went on point, collected hounds, carried on as if I was riding a horse who had been normal all his life, with everything in his brain working exactly as it should.

Then the fuse blew.

For an instant, he lost control and started to bolt.

But then, somehow, the fuse seemed to automatically repair itself.

This occurred three or four times and soon my fingers were crossed so hard it hurt. At the end of the day, though, all was well. It seemed as if we - Lavender, Morag, Kate Solisti and I - had nearly cracked it. Nod was firing on all cylinders, and came home head held up on high - magic, pure undiluted magic! But the final test would be the following Monday. Was everything going to hold under the ultimate examination?

The big day came. The meet was at friends George and Virginia Scott Watson's farm, Easter Softlaw, just a mile and a half away. Virginia and two of their sons would be hunting.

"Nod," I told him, "you are in charge today. You will have these fast galloping horses behind you, and you will have to lead the way, jump all the fences, be instantly responsive to instructions from me and be in full control of yourself. Understood?"

Anxious but excited, I rode to the meet in brilliant sunshine, where I found about fifty people on horseback and a hundred on foot, most of whom would be following in eighty or so cars. Having partaken of a sausage, sausage roll, delicious fruitcake and a glass of port - Nod, poor fellow having to make do with grass - we were ready for the off. The day went like a dream. Nod was filled with the exhilaration of an explosive self-controlled power and I could tell from his assuredness that all was well. This was not a mere red-letter day; this was something far, far better - a diamond-encrusted-letter day - perhaps? Whatever, I was in heaven, I was walking above the clouds, on top of the world. Nod had at last achieved a full recovery. The aura, the radiance shining from him that day was amazing. He could not stop shouting to the horse world "I've done it! I've done it!"

Near the end of the day, as we galloped through a farm steading while hunting a fox from the Kale River towards the Bowmont Forest, a cry went up: "Loose horse." It seemed that the runaway had heard Nod and was determined to attract attention to itself. Fully clothed in its New Zealand rug, it had jumped out of its field and dashed off into Bowmont Forest. I dispatched one of the mounted followers to catch and return it and that evening the owners rang me. What was the situation if their horse had been damaged? They asked. Or the rugs? I explained that all hunts have to carry very substantial public liability insurance. Thankfully for all parties concerned, though, it wasn't needed in this instance. As our conversation continued, I learnt that their horse was called Duchess and they explained that they were experiencing problems with her. Ah, I thought, now we are coming to the real reason for the phone call.

Duchess had gone AWOL to be noticed and her cry for help had given her owners the opportunity to contact me. Seemingly, Duchess box-walked and they had gone to very considerable trouble and expense to provide her with an excellent selection of New Zealand rugs so that, even though being trace-high clipped, she could live outside very comfortably in all weathers day and night. As they explained this problem, it rang a bell in my memory.

The first hunter I had ridden as a teenager, having outgrown ponies, was an old horse of my father's called Volcano, who had been bred locally at Muirhouselaw. I can still remember my first day's hunting with him. The hounds had found in Eastfield Whins and they followed the fox travelling south. I rode back to the road, turned right and had planned to go sixty yards then turn left through a gate off this road and head for Kippilaw. Volcano had a different plan. I had both hands on the left-hand rein as we approached the gate, his head was bent round to the left, but his legs were going straight on.

From his left eye the message came loud and clear: "Boy, I know much more about this hunting lark than you. I am going straight on and jump that fence off the road and you can please yourself."

With a quick injection of common sense I dropped the left-hand rein and we jumped together off the road.

Volcano rested during the day. At night, though, it was a different matter. He walked so much that he had actually worn a circle in the concrete floor of his box at Monksford, pounding round and round.

Duchess had obviously heard Nod's repeated cries of " I've done it! At last I am healed!" and thought, "Hey, I'll have some of that. I need assistance to heal, too."

But had Volcano, in this lifetime now Duchess, recognised me? My debt to Volcano for looking after me so well as a teenager could be repaid by going to help him/her now. So I arranged to visit Duchess. I inspected her and was shown all her fabulous New Zealand rugs. We then went and looked at her stables, where I saw a lovely big box, immaculately tidy with whitewashed walls, but with a dark, lofty and oppressive roof. A problem there, perhaps? I asked Duchess what was troubling her.

She showed me a scene from a past life in which the landscape resembled parts of India. "I was killed by a big cat, a tiger," she told me telepathically. But that was it and as I couldn't glean any more information to help solve the mystery, I rang Morag. I had found that our combined effort was greater than the sum of our individual efforts in unravelling these enigmas.

The story that was eventually revealed concerned Duchess's life as a workhorse on a peasant farm. Here her two principal jobs were to spend all day walking round and round driving either the corn mill or the irrigation wheel. The poor farmer's only children were twin daughters, who although no more than twelve, were required to help with the work. The village priest wanted these girls, particularly because they were twins, to live and serve in the temple. The farmer was extremely upset about this, he hated the idea of his daughters becoming serving girls in the temple. He was at his wits' end, with no one he could turn to for help. The village headman hadn't the authority to override the priest and the priest was absolutely determined that he was going to have the twins. The farmer, in desperation so rather than having his girls confiscated, took the twins deep into the forest and tied them up in a sinister glen where no light penetrated because of the heavy overhang of foliage. Then he hid close by and waited. The girls realised what their father had done and a burning anger flared up inside them against him, but it was too late - a tiger found the bait and killed the girls. When the priest discovered what the farmer had done, he was furious, speechless in temper, and decided to take the poor man's worn-out old exhausted horse and use it as bait for the tiger, instead of a goat as normal. That also meant that the farmer would be incapable of working his holding. The priest took the horse out to the same spooky glen with its thick forest canopy and tied it up. The tiger came and killed the horse and in turn the tiger was killed.

Now that Duchess had regurgitated this horrific tale from her subconscience, it was necessary to explain to her that it was irrelevant to her for evermore, and that she could erase it from her memory bank. The trauma gone, Duchess ceased to box walk, and my debt to Volcano had been honoured.

It is just so difficult to explain in words the sheer pleasure and glow one feels, from being the instrument in assisting these quite wonderful people on four legs to heal. That Monday was not merely the culmination of three and a half years of not-so-patient work on Nod by the team, but Nod and I had been the catalyst, which had allowed Duchess to wave the flag with *help* printed on it. And as a result, I was able to repay with thanks what Volcano had done for me when I was a child.

Nod and I had a few more days hunting together, before the New Year's Day meet in the Square in Kelso. This was such a blissful period, filled with so many magic moments, but at the back of my mind lurked a premonition. Something was forewarning me that now success had been achieved, we were not to have a long and happy time together in this life.

Come New Year's Day, I was on duty so Nod would be Field Master. The ground had a light dusting of snow but underneath it was quite soft. I asked Gillian, the elder of the two sisters who helped in the summer, if she could ride second horse to me on Morris. This was just a pretend question as there was no way she would have been allowed on Nod. Gillian was so excited with this prospect that she was instantly speechless. She was the first of several children that Morris had taught to ride and taken for their first day's hunting.

Nod was particularly strong that day, because whilst he was gaffer, he also had to show off to the 'little man' Morris that he was the most powerful horse in the world. I did not have an easy ride! He just switched on the turbo chargers, and at one stage as we galloped through a very deep, sticky ploughed field, he refused to slacken, treated it as if he was galloping on the top of firm old grass. Twelve days later, out hunting, the result of that behaviour showed up; a stress fracture in his cannon bone. He had been perfectly sound on exercise until then. Whilst he recuperated, Karen, Gillian's sister and his favourite girlfriend, made him a special get well card. With the aid of radionics, arnica, symphitum (comfrey), willow bark, meadowsweet and nettle, the fracture took some months to heal.

I hoped that Nod had learnt not to show off, but somehow doubted it.

Chapter 12

Cats and Quizzy arrive

Nod, along with Milly and Morris, went out for their summer holidays. JoJo went to her lovely retirement home in Dumfriesshire. I thought that I would have an economy drive and see if the three horses would manage next season, so made no provisions about finding a fourth horse. Now that Nod was hunky-dory and able to field master, surely I would be able to cope? However there was just the faintest niggle at the back of my mind over my premonition and he had injured himself that day on the 1st January 1997.

The season duly started and all seemed to be going well. My misgivings wouldn't go away though. One morning in September after the meet at Satchells, I had just finished putting people in the position I wanted and looked around to check that everything was in order, when I spotted a horse, that I hadn't seen at the meet or ever before. About fifty yards away, the horse - a mare - turned her head towards me and shouted, "Hi, here I am, I am your next horse."

Now, I don't believe in such a thing as 'coincidence' and so I transmitted the somewhat muted reply "OK, but I can't do anything about it now, be patient."

I knew that the man who was riding the mare that morning was a part time dealer. So I rang him to enquire about the horse. She was a five-year-old dark bay called Fat Cat, and had been bred and broken by a lady and her daughter near Bridge of Earn with the intention of performing dressage on her as her dad was a Dutch warm blood. Sadly they had forgotten to consult the horse. She had become completely bored with dressage, which didn't allow her to let off steam and her personality had turned stroppy and bad mannered. Now they were unable to handle her and when they put a saddle on her in the stables she started to buck and just barged over them. She had obviously totally outgrown her home and had unfortunately found out how strong she was. When I had a chance to look at her in more detail, I could see she was a big-boned scopey mare with a long back, so she would have a raking stride, also there was a bucking bump on her back. One front hoof slightly malformed, which could have been corrected as a foal by remedial shoeing, but she was a real workman-like horse. And it was quickly evident that she had a definite mind of her own. That morning, when she attracted my attention, was the first time she had seen hounds or any form of hunting - let alone big wide-open spaces. Yet she appeared to handle the situation like an old stager.

As she wasn't fit I arranged that I would wait until early in October before I would try her out hunting. This was done from the Houdshall meet, and part way through the morning I swapped from Milly onto Fat Cat. Almost immediately, we meet a solid timber fence inclining backwards at an awkward angle, not a nice obstacle for a novice horse. But there was no hesitation from her, straight over she went and further I felt completely confident that she was going to jump. As the morning wore on, it became obvious that not only was she a natural, but she was a front runner, like Ben. No way would she tolerate horses in front of her - she was the herd leader. I remember one occasion when I visited a neighbouring pack with Ben - never again. I tried to keep him in with the rest of the horses, but after barely half a mile he couldn't contain himself any longer and bolted straight through them all and up to the front. In his mind that settled that silly nonsense - I go number one. Fat Cat had exactly the same idea. All the furore and hassle she put the women up north through was forgotten. This hunting work was ideal for her - she loved it.

I decided there and then to buy Cats, as I named her, because the last thing she was, was a fat cat. However, to begin with I had no room at home, so Cats had to go to a livery yard.

Some weeks later, I heard that the excellent animal communicator Nicci Mackay was touring Scotland. She has a similar gift as Kate Solisti. So because I was still experiencing problems with Milly blowing hot and cold on her willingness to perform consistently, and neither Morag nor I could get any more information from her. I thought that it would be a good idea if Nicci talked with Milly to see if she could get an alternative lead. Also, the people at the livery yard were experiencing considerable problems with Cats. When Dave the farrier had been shoeing her, she had a go at him - not how to make friends! So perhaps Nicci could do something for my new horse too.

Nicci picked up from Milly how sore her fetlocks were. I had realised that she had this peculiarity of equal-sized hooves, which were all smaller than you would have expected on a horse of her size. But to complain that her fetlocks weren't strong enough to carry out the necessary workload was a bit of a stopper and I could think of no solution to that problem.

Cats, however, told Nicci that she realised now how naughty she had been at her original home. She further thought that if she behaved really well at the livery yard she would be sent back there. So far she hadn't demonstrated any inclination to turn that thought into practice and never did.

Trouble struck again during the Stoisley crossroads day on the 1st of November. Nod sustained a fracture in his near fore fetlock. After several weeks rest he appeared to be sound so I took him out again. With his adrenaline flowing, you would not have been able to detect that anything was wrong, but I wasn't convinced so came home early. I arranged for him to have a holiday with Morag, thereby also ensuring that I couldn't be tempted to go hunting with him too quickly. Morag had access to some boxes in a lovely old-fashioned stone-built square yard on the west side of the Edinburgh/ Glasgow motorway, which had a much nicer and warmer atmosphere than where she had previously been. After he had healed, Morag started to exercise Nod. Once when, she galloped him and after having been run away with, she decided that perhaps that wasn't such a clever idea after all. Well, let's face it, he was a man's horse and he was feeling great.

Amongst all his luggage was his pink rock and a new set of shoes, to save Morag's farrier the trouble of measuring and fitting if needed, which they weren't.

To help Milly recover from the pain in her fetlocks, when Nod was ready to come home, I swapped them around so she had a holiday with Morag.

You will recall in one of Milly's past lives she had complained about having her foal taken away from her by a farming couple and how extremely upset she was over this and very annoyed that, to compound the issue, they had not looked after her foal correctly. She had totally trusted this couple and they were good stockmen. Well, when Milly was with Morag, she kept on harping on "I want a foal. I want a foal." Then a girl from the West of Scotland came to have a healing session with Morag. This girl had no contact in her life with horses, no experience or knowledge of horses and yet all she could talk to Morag about was a mare. She described this horse in minute detail and the picture she painted was Milly to a tee, a few days after Morag told me this story, this was the picture revealed to me.

I was the farmer and the girl from the West of Scotland was my wife in that lifetime. Milly was a much heavier-built mare then and she would have been ridden as required, also pulling light carts and implements for simple farm work. She had been covered by a Connemara-type pony stallion, in the hope that she would throw a better quality riding horse than she was herself. The foal had been born successfully but was found to have deformed fetlock joints and would never be able to stand properly or walk. So, even before Milly was able to clean it up, I had no alternative but to remove the foal, take it outside and shoot it. I have tried to explain to Milly why this was necessary, but she is still not inclined to believe me, the break of trust was so severe.

Before this tale came out of the woodwork, Milly, being so pretty and dainty, never rolled in mud or dirt, only on clean grass. But after this story was revealed, Milly went out and rolled in the dirtiest, muddiest patch she could find and continued to do so. I never understood why?

After Nod came home his shoes wore out, so I rang Dave the farrier, only to find that he was off work having had an accident when paring a two-year old's hooves. The horse had jerked and his knife had penetrated his protective leather apron and sliced into his knee -

hellish. So, knowing that I had the unused set of shoes that Nod came back with from his holidays, I rang North Northumberland blacksmiths, who duly had their passports stamped and came over the border. I gave them the shoes, but they took one look and announced superiorly that they wouldn't fit Nod. Funny, they had for five years! Anyway, they proceeded to fit their own. Were Nod's 'holiday' shoes ever going to be put on?

Early in December a friend in the south rang to say that she had a seven-year-old grey mare for sale. Was I interested? I thought flipping heck, I don't want or need a fifth horse. I had started the season attempting an economy drive and now it looked as though I was being sent another horse. Totally gullible, or open to the soft sell - I'm not sure which describes me better - but my gut feeling told me that this horse was to come here. Hence the next thing I knew, here was this completely green, uneducated horse called Quizzical Creek, Quizzy for short, arriving to join the team. When she came off the wagon here, I saw a white not a grey horse, because besides having white hair and hooves her skin was pink - but she was not an albino. About 16.2, well built, good bone, up to weight and with no blemishes; but I wondered what all her problems were. What made it so imperative that she arranged to come to me?

I found out very quickly that she was well named, quite the most inquisitive horse I have ever come across. Also her tummy was extremely close to her heart!

Luckily extra help with the horses was on hand. When Nod went on holiday, I had just Susan, who lived on the farm and helped in the big farmhouse, with their children plus their ponies. Jane appeared out of the blue. Her parents had recently retired and moved into the village that lies immediately below the farm. After completing a degree course in horse management at Kentucky University, Jane spent six months at Monty Robert's establishment. She had returned some months previously and assisted her parents in their move and then found some work with horses for a lady in the village. But now she had some spare time on her hands and had called around to see if I needed help with the horses.

Once I'd heard all about her background, I replied, "Great, yes, I do need some help. I think you'll find that working here will be tantamount to adding a PhD to the degree you all ready have. I'll set the exam in the summer."

Jane looked completely nonplussed. So I explained that whilst Monty Roberts communicated with horses by body language - what he calls 'equus'- I and others communicate by telepathy and on a soul-to-soul basis, thus enabling us to read past life traumas. She nodded, but I could tell she had only half taken in what I'd said. "Don't worry," I told her, "I'll explain more to you as we go along." I introduced her to Susan and left them chattering happily.

During the time that Milly was on holiday with Morag near Edinburgh, the hay shed next to the stables became empty, so two temporary loose boxes could be made in it. This allowed me to bring Cats home, she had continued to give the livery yard some grief- so much for her idea of behaving well and been taken back to her original home. But Cats was such a dominant matriarchal mare that not only had she sussed out the pecking order amongst horses, but she was also pretty canny when it came to summing up humans. Those of a lower level were to be bossed about like any horse, it seemed. When I had a man as a groom for one winter, she dropped him on top of a hedge one day on exercise and galloped home. Thereafter he was never allowed by her to put a bridle on her. "You, man are only here to see that my bedroom is kept tidy!" She settled in here next to Nod straight away.

Dave and I continued to have problems with Cats when she was being shod. She seemed to have particularly sensitive front hooves, especially the near side one, which was malformed, it would have been better if she had had remedial farrier work on that hoof as a youngster - even the clinches hurt her. So in an effort to help her I called up the angels for assistance and I watched as they took the nail off the near side hoof and massaged the bones, then rearranged them so there was slightly more space between them and put the nail back on. Months later, because I continued to find that Cats was unexplainably having problems with her near side shoulder, I phoned Kate Solisti to see if there was anything she could pick up. This is Kate's reply:

FAX TO: Peter Neilson 011 44 1573 22 4146.
FROM: Kate Solisti-Mattelon phone 505 466-6958.
SUBJECT: Conversation with Cats.
DATE: December 29, 1999.
Here's what Cats has to tell you through me.

First, Nod would like to come through. He says that he has been talking with Cats, explaining that it's better to be straightforward with you about everything He told her, "It took me the longest time to tell Peter the core of my problem. I, like you, was afraid to let him down, to disappoint him. I wanted to give everything to Peter, my body and soul, as I knew that we were one. I struggled with my fear and pain for so long When I finally told him, it was a gentle breakthrough. It was not at all what I expected. It was a release of tremendous proportions, but it was quiet like a breeze. Nothing like the hurricane of emotions I thought it would be. I felt his tremendous love for me wash over me and I knew that everything, EVERYTHING - past, present and future would be right again."

Cats said, "I was afraid, just as Nod felt afraid. I have been so happy, so overjoyed hunting, as you know. The exhilaration of the hunt suits me perfectly. I feel as if I have been a hunter forever, and I feel free, perfect, at one with everything when I hunt. My shoulder problem is connected with my entire near fore leg. I like Nod, I have a memory I have not wanted to share, or better yet, have been afraid to share. I have wanted to scream out my shame for months, but have been afraid.

In a lifetime before this one, I was in a stablefire. I was a work horse of large proportions. I worked as a team with my sister who was not quite as strong as I. In our stable were the racehorses as well. The thoroughbreds were more highly valued than we. I was jealous. When the fire started, I calculated, albeit slowly, how to break myself and my sister free and leave the others behind. It was a cruel, selfish thought, but it consumed me, even as the others cried for help. I used my near fore shoulder to push the wooden wall of my stall. It gave me more resistance than I expected. The fire gained intensity. My sister called to me, worried. I told her not to worry, we would soon be free. Other horses were being overcome with smoke. I pushed and pushed, ramming my shoulder into the wall. At last, it gave way. Collie (my sister) and I ran out into the cool night.

We watched as people came to put out the fire and rescue the thoroughbreds. I knew they thought only of the thoroughbreds and nothing of Collie and me. I was angry and glad that I had saved only us. Then I looked at Collie. Kind soul, that she had always been, she shook in terror and sadness as people ran about while the fire raged and horses screamed.

She looked at me and said, "What have you done? If I had died, panic and pained in that fire, you would feel my pain, my sorrow as I now feel for the others. I shall never be the same knowing what you chose to do."

From that point on she never spoke to me again. We worked side by side for ten more years and she never spoke another word. I begged for her forgiveness, but she would not speak. When she died, I was with her. She looked into my eyes and told me that she loved me. Then she died. That moment was filled with the most inexplicable grief and anger at myself. I vowed to myself that I should never again deserve to feel joy, to be happy. I went to my grave with this self-inflicted punishment."

At this moment, I (Kate) tenderly asked Cats if she could forgive herself as Collie had done. Cats said, "Peter, Peter, do I deserve happiness? I know what your answer is. I am ready to begin to release my vow."

She said, "I will need help passing through the fire and meeting with the horses that died because I didn't help them. I need their forgiveness, just as I need to forgive myself."

Oh Gosh, Collie is coming in. She says, "I am here to speak to my beloved Cats, but I wish you to hear what I have to say. My Dearest, it is time to embrace life. The jealousies of the past are shadows of another time. In this lifetime you are generous, loving, beautiful. You have the most exquisitely beautiful body (in my eyes). You are no longer confined to pull a plow or wagon, you are free to fly through the fields! Do you not see that the Creator has forgiven you and given you a great gift? It would be a tragedy indeed for you not to fully enjoy this gift of great joy and freedom. You have been forgiven by all. Now you must forgive yourself and on with living!!"

Cats: "I hear you, my Heart, my Beloved. I need some time to integrate all that has happened this evening Peter, I understand now. I am so grateful for your help in holding the energy for me to reach myself and Collie. I am grateful for the opportunity to share my story. I am beyond gratitude for receiving Collie's and Nod's messages. I wish to be whole again and to "fly through the fields," as Collie said I must do.

I would like to experience the Angelic healing again. I think my body will respond quite differently now, for I am willing to be well in my shoulder and near fore. I don't think the distortion in my hoof will prevent me from being sound, once I have accepted that it is correct for me to be so. I will work hard with the angels to release my old self-punishment and embrace vibrant health, balance and wholeness. Thankyou."

Wow. Well Peter, this is what I received. Although, as I reread what I wrote, the huge emotions Cats, Collie and Nod felt as they spoke can't by fully conveyed in words, I know though, from your experience, you will tune in and feel what I felt.

I dearly hope and pray that Cats can forgive herself and allow herself to be well and whole so that she can "fly through the fields" once more. Please keep me informed of her progress. I think that its marvellous that she has shared all this before the new year. She will be able to have a really fresh start now.

Morris, Quizzy, Jane and Cats

Stable Plan

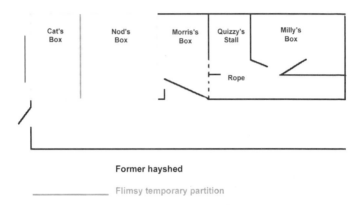

Former hayshed

———————————— Flimsy temporary partition

Stable Plan (Nod's and Cats' boxes being where the hay had been).

Cats, after recounting this traumatic tale, has not had any problems with her shoulder. Further, some months before she told this story, a friend visited a yard, south of here and phoned to say, that she'd just seen a horse with a label around it's neck reading 'Neilson'. I rang the yard and bought the horse, which they delivered within days on their journey northwards to a horse trial. (Actually they couldn't believe that I would buy a horse unseen and unveted, thus wished to be shot of her as soon as possible before I changed my mind). Hence a dapple-grey mare called Penny arrived here. Penny was Cat's sister Collie.

As for Quizzy, the standard procedure was carried out with a small sample piece of her mane being posted to Lavender. As normal she popped the witness on her instrument to see what she could discover, then rang me to say that Quizzy had a fault in the cartilage in the scapula. I had not found this, but it did explain why she had a concave muscle on the near side of her chest. It had, though, become noticeable very quickly that she was a neurotic bag of nerves. Not surprising that she came to me.... As well as her bad nerves, she had no self-confidence, if you did not instantly tie her up having put the bridle on, she would have chewed through both reins - and the farting was something to be believed. You could be standing at the side of her in the stables and she would drop on the ground, suffering from colic. That first winter Quizzy developed colic about thirty five times and if I had not known how to stop it with my hands, I dread to think what the vet's bills would have been. Linda Tellington-Jones explains how to do it in her book *Getting in Touch with Horses*, but please call your vet first. I had to put Quizzy in a straight bar bit with long cheek pieces because she was able to get the snaffle rings into her mouth. She was taken hunting as much as possible, ridden by Jane, with me on another horse, in an attempt to bolster her confidence by always having a stable companion. Very rarely did I field master on her and then only in an area where there was no jumping. She was not the bravest of souls. Definitely bottom of the pecking order, but so inquisitive! The year after Quizzy was put down, because of degenerating bones, I discovered that the cause of these problems were because she had been slightly brain damaged at birth. Also in a past life she had been Bucephalus, Alexander the Great's famous horse.

Nod started to go lame after hunting. Oh dear, it never rained but it poured - now what had gone wrong? I couldn't find the answer and this was both upsetting and puzzling. Eventually I realised that it was his offside sacro-iliac joint that was in trouble, the worst designed joints that a horse has. Damn and bugger. Was my premonition coming home to roost? I called another healer, Sue Connelly and told her this was the third physical problem that Nod has experienced since his major mental healing, please, was there anyway she could help his sacro-iliac joint? Sue was able to pick up that this accident had been caused when people were trying to train Nod to be ridden. In an effort to master him, they had pulled him over backwards, thus causing the injury. Thankfully, through the power of thought, Sue was able to heal the joint, in the opposite way to which she is able to burn off splints.

Quizzy

Chapter 13

Nod and I are a centaur

Suddenly lots of consecutive events took place, for which I can give no rational explanation, but they were stirring up energy levels. On Thursday 26th February 1998 between 5.25pm. and 6.30pm., there was a total solar eclipse. On the same day between 6.10pm. and 6.30pm., beacons were lit all over the United Kingdom, this being the old system of warning the country that the enemy has attacked. On Sunday 1st March there was a massive march in London.

The next day Nod and Quizzy were getting ready to go hunting. Jane had groomed, tacked and rugged Nod and had started on Quizzy. Susan was mucking-out Cats in the next door box when, to her surprise, Nod went down and rolled. Nod loved to roll, in the field with or without his New Zealand rug, after hunting in the stables, but never before had he done so when ready and waiting to go hunting. Susan shouted at him and told him to get up. This he did, whereupon she remarked, "What a mess you have got yourself into. Look at you, shavings everywhere, in your mane, under your rug. What are you playing at?"

Nod was not bothered. He looked at her with faint disdain and a twinge of surprise, raised a haughty expression and replied, "Well, she can jolly well tidy me up again, can't she?"

Nod was so totally relaxed out hunting that day. While concentrating solely on hounds and hunting, he was so easy to ride; in fact the easiest he had ever been - a dream. It appeared as if he no longer had to prove that he was 'Top Horse' by blasting everyone off the park. Though his power and speed was undiminished he was totally self-controlled. I talked to him aloud much more than normal, but we were also having two-way thought transmission. I did not need to ride using any aids, no legs, no hands, yes no hands. We read each other's thoughts, they were synchronised.

We were as one: a Centaur.

Some while back in one of his communications with Kate Solisti, Nod had asked if I could "ride him without hands", a request that caused much sarcastic mirth! And now it had been achieved - a bigger success than climbing Everest. But it was the calm before the storm.

We had been galloping through knee-deep heather on the third Eildon Hill and slowed to a stop to look down onto the woods and listen to the music of the hounds. Then, without warning, Nod keeled over, crashed sideways into Quizzy. He went down, got up, went down again. It seemed obvious to me that he'd had a heart attack. On my knees, with tears streaming down my face, I cradled his head in my hands as his life ebbed quietly away.

Devastated, I returned home with Quizzy, who was strangely subdued. The stables were very quiet and sombre; the horses realised that Nod had passed on.

There was no happy chatter. Nod's tack was given an extra special clean and polished and hung up, a dark saddlecloth being hung over his saddle. Almost total quiet prevailed; all that could be heard was that loveliest of sounds. Munch, crunch, the hayracks were being emptied. Munch, crunch.

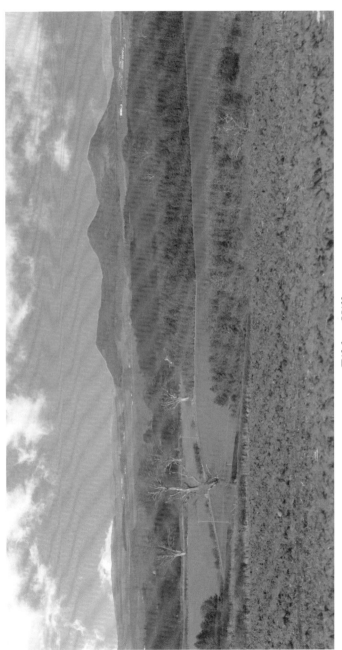

Eildon Hills

Chapter 14

The spirit World's celebration to honour Nod

With Nod's box vacant, Cats, in her effort to see out of the door, would have broken down the flimsy partition. Horses do not like to move straight away into another horse's space and though Nod's box was physically empty, to Cats it was still his; or so I thought. I knew that if I moved one of the other horses into Nod's box in order to keep Cats company, then all the horses would have been unsettled and particularly the one in Nod's space. But I was forgetting that when a horse dies, it will arrange for a replacement to come to the bereft owner. Now, we humans are free to choose and in our superior way think we know best, so often reject the horse selected for us.

I realised then that Nod had known for sometime that he was going to move on. He had already called forward his replacement - Cats. It was safe, right and proper to move her into his box. Peace reigned. Munch, crunch.

With no knowledge of hunting, Cats had taken to it like a duck to water. She was a natural. In fact in a previous conversation with Kate Solisti she had told Kate that in none of her lives had she been a hunter and thought that it was definitely the most wonderful life she had experienced.

I have no doubt that all was totally preordained, even to the extent that Nod's collapse had taken place in deep heather, so no body damage was incurred by either of us, with him passing on unblemished to the music of the hounds. I had carried out my job of healing Nod and he had taught me about the spiritual side of healing. It was enormously significant to me that Nod had left this world on the Eildon Hills. A place where I had spent many hours riding as a child - I had lost my first bowler hat on them whilst out hunting - and now, from here, he could survey the land over which he had jurisdiction. The Eildon Hills are very important spiritually and what with the strange energy patterns that had occurred a few days before, then the massive march in London, it was now to be the turn of the Spirits.

On entering the house, I rang Lavender and Morag and faxed Kate with the news. Some hours later Morag rang back.

"You will have to go back up the Eildon Hills," she said "Nod is stuck there and the spirits are celebrating."

Then I saw what was happening - the word 'celebrating' wasn't anywhere near powerful enough for what the spirits were doing.

Twenty four hours later I went back, climbing with my four dogs to the spot where Nod had died. His body had been removed the previous evening. Nod's spirit was standing where he had fallen, on duty looking out over the land. His passing away had caused a phenomenal, joyous celebration by the spirits; there were no acts of grieving or mourning, just celebration. The spirits of hundreds of thousands of warriors, soldiers, horses, mules, camels, oxen and donkeys had come to honour Nod - the WAR HORSE. There was no funeral march, no dirges, just joyous hailing of the safe return of the healed hero. Bands played, drums rolled, trumpets of brass, shell and horn blew, cymbals clashed, pipes squealed. The noise surged and bellowed out to the world. Soldiers in all their different uniforms were there, Terra Cotta army, Roman army, Japanese Middle Ages army, Bedouins in flowing white robes, Peninsula War army. The Battalions, Regiments, Brigades, Divisions paraded and marched past Nod. They saluted, clashed their swords against their shields, lifted the spears aloft, fired their muzzleloaders, muskets, revolvers, rifles, cannons and mortars. The cavalry wheeled past, the baggage trains lumbered by.

They celebrated and saluted the return of the healed War Horse - Nod.

I told Nod to stand down and returned his spirit to God.

I love Nod.

I am White Horse of the Cherokee Nation.

Glossary

Angleberries	Warts or Sarcoids.
Arnica	Herbal/homeopathic treatment for wounds, bruises and many other types of injury.
Box	Stable for a horse, in America you would call a box a stall.
Box walking	This is when a horse continues to walk non stop in its box/stall.
Bucking bump	A bump in the horse's spine just behind the saddle.
Catherine Rommelaere	Author on horses in ancient Egypt.
Centaur	A horse with a human body, arms and head in place of its neck and head.
Comfrey	Herb which helps fractured bones to heal.
Cub hunting	Start of hunting season when young hounds are trained to only follow the scent of foxes.
Dutch warm blood	Breed of horse originally from the European continent.

Edgar Cayce	An American, who under hypnosis, carried out past live regression and communicated with the angelic world.
Eton beagles	Eton College own a pack of beagles which are looked after by the students.
Field	The collective name for all the riders and horses following hounds.
Field Master	The person in charge of seeing that the 'field' go the correct way out hunting.
Hackamore	A bitless bridle, which exerts pressure on the horse's nostril to control it.
Hill topping	When you follow hounds not with the 'field' but at a distance.
Hodden doune	Overcome by stress and strain.
Kate Solisti-Mattelon	An American animal communicator and healer.
Lavender Dower	Co-founder of radionic therapy in the UK.

Linda Tellington-Jones	An American internationally recognised horse expert who created a holistic technique that promotes healing and founded T.T.E.A.M.
Meadowsweet	Herbal treatment for use as an anti-inflammatory.
Meet	The assembly place for a day's hunting.
Monty Roberts	An American horsewhisperer.
Morag MacDonald-Worsley	A Scottish spiritual healer.
Nettle	Herbal addition to daily feed, being rich in minerals.
Nicci Mackay	An English animal communicator.
Old stager	An experienced person, old hand.
Peesies	A Scottish word for Peewits or Lapwings.
Puppy show	A show when the previous year's puppies are shown prior to them starting their hunting careers.
Raking stride	When a horse has an exceptionally long stride when galloping.

Raven	The largest member of the crow family.
Reactor panel saddle	A saddle similar on top to our conventional saddles, but underneath are two flexible panels which take up the shape of the horse's back and spreads the rider's weight over two and half times the area of a normal saddle.
Regumate	Veterinary prescription for Mares who have difficult or irregular seasons.
Sacro-iliac joint	The joint at the top of horses' hind legs.
Scapula	Shoulder-blade.
Snaffle	A bit with rings on the outside and jointed in the middle.
Staleing	When a horse passes urine.
Stall	An area separated by partitions, six feet apart, which is stabling for a horse with a manger and hayrack at the front to which the horse is attached by a rope, the back being open.
Steading	A farmyard.
Sue Connelly	A healer.

Symbiosis	Association of two different organisms attached to each other.
To nap	When a horse in motion performs dishonestly.
Thuja	Homeopathic treatment for angleberries.
Trace high clip	When a horse's tummy is clipped up to where the shafts of a cart would be.
T.T.E.A.M.	Tellington Touch Equine Awareness Method.
Vic	Cream to relieve restricted breathing.
Waterloo Cup	The premier greyhound coursing competition.
Whaups	Curlews.
Whipper-ins	Assistants who help the huntsman.
White horses	Technically all grey or white horses are referred to as "grey." But to be more descriptive of Quizzy I called her white.
Willow Bark	Nature's painkiller.

Map

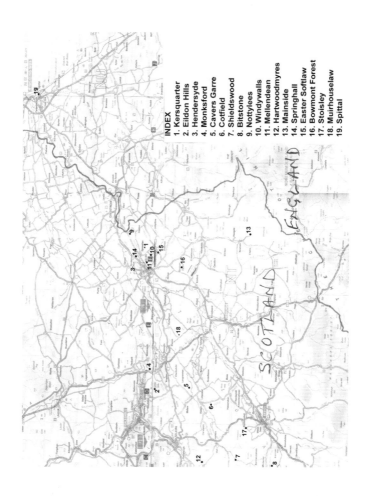

INDEX
1. Kersquarter
2. Eildon Hills
3. Hendersyde
4. Monksford
5. Cavers Garre
6. Cotfield
7. Shieldswood
8. Bitstone
9. Nottylees
10. Windywalls
11. Mellendean
12. Hartwoodmyres
13. Mainside
14. Springhall
15. Easter Softlaw
16. Bowmont Forest
17. Stoisley
18. Muirhouselaw
19. Spittal

About the Author

Peter Neilson

He had a conventional childhood from a farming background surrounded by horses and dogs in Scotland. He qualified as a mechanical engineer but after twenty years in industry he took up farming, a diabolically wet summer destroyed his harvest and farming. For fifteen years he was a Joint Master of the Duke of Buccleuch's Hunt. When he purchased a new horse "Nod", he discovered that Nod was a mentally traumatised horse. So he set off on a journey to attempt to heal Nod. His work has been the subject of great media and public interest and has featured on BBC, Channel 4 and Border TV as well as the printed media.